COMPENDIUM OF
METAPHYSICS III

THE HUMAN BEING - EVOLUTION OF FORM, AWAKENING OF CONSCIOUSNESS - MEDITATION

Other Books by Adriana Balthazar MD, PhD

-44 Spiritual Poems and Metaphysical Commentaries (co-authored with Reshma Ali)

-The Western Book of Death

-Compendium of Metaphysics I: The Human Being – Physical and Etheric Bodies

-Compendium of Metaphysics II: The Human Being – Emotional, Lower Mental, and Spiritual Bodies

COMPENDIUM OF METAPHYSICS III

THE HUMAN BEING - EVOLUTION OF FORM, AWAKENING OF CONSCIOUSNESS - MEDITATION

ADRIANA BALTHAZAR, MD; Ph.D.

Balboa Press books may be ordered through booksellers or by contacting:

Balboa Press
A Division of Hay House
1663 Liberty Drive
Bloomington, IN 47403
www.balboapress.com
1 (877) 407-4847

Because of the dynamic nature of the Internet, any web addresses or links contained in this book may have changed since publication and may no longer be valid. The views expressed in this work are solely those of the author and do not necessarily reflect the views of the publisher, and the publisher hereby disclaims any responsibility for them.

Any people depicted in stock imagery provided by Getty Images are models, and such images are being used for illustrative purposes only.
Certain stock imagery © Getty Images.

ISBN: 978-1-9822-4750-8 (sc)
ISBN: 978-1-9822-4751-5 (e)

Library of Congress Control Number: 2020909546

Print information available on the last page.

Balboa Press rev. date: 06/03/2020

A DIVISION OF HAY HOUSE

CONTENTS

DIAGRAM #1
The Real Constitution of Human Beings

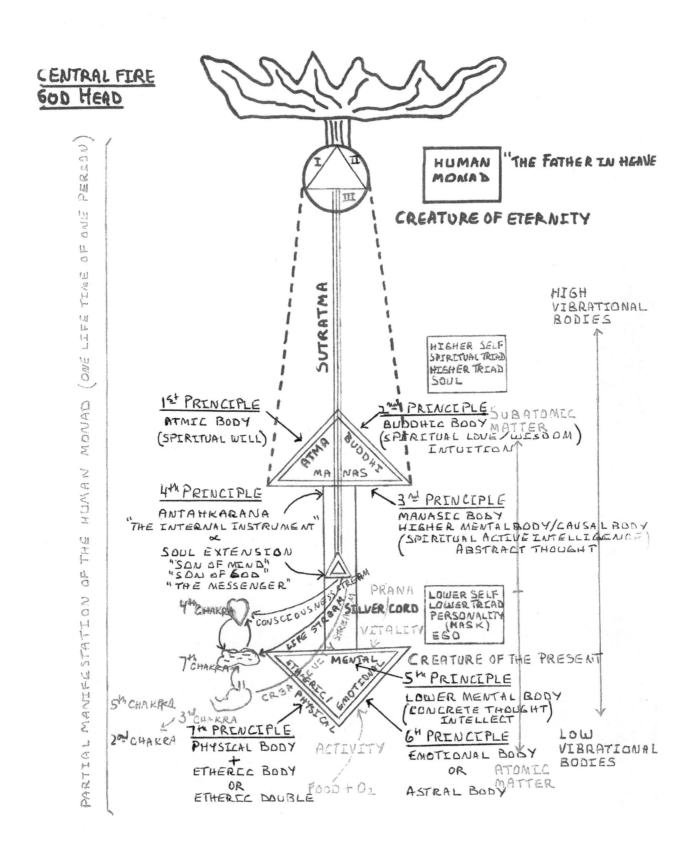

CENTRAL FIRE
GOD HEAD

PARTIAL MANIFESTATION OF THE HUMAN MONAD (ONE LIFE TIME OF ONE PERSON)

HUMAN MONAD — "THE FATHER IN HEAVE

CREATURE OF ETERNITY

SUTRATMA

HIGH VIBRATIONAL BODIES

HIGHER SELF
SPIRITUAL TRIAD
HIGHER TRIAD
SOUL

1st PRINCIPLE
ATMIC BODY
(SPIRITUAL WILL)

2nd PRINCIPLE
BUDDHIC BODY
(SPIRITUAL LOVE/WISDOM)
INTUITION

SUBATOMIC MATTER

ATMA BUDDHI MANAS

4th PRINCIPLE
ANTAHKARANA
"THE INTERNAL INSTRUMENT"
&
SOUL EXTENSION
"SON OF MIND"
"SON OF GOD"
"THE MESSENGER"

3rd PRINCIPLE
MANASIC BODY
HIGHER MENTAL BODY/CAUSAL BODY
(SPIRITUAL ACTIVE INTELLIGENCE)
ABSTRACT THOUGHT

4th CHAKRA

CONSCIOUSNESS STREAM

LIFE STREAM

STRENGTH

PRANA
SILVER CORD
VITALITY

LOWER SELF
LOWER TRIAD
PERSONALITY
(MASK)
EGO

7th CHAKRA

ETHERIC

CREA

PHYSICAL

MENTAL

EMOTIONAL

CREATURE OF THE PRESENT

5th PRINCIPLE
LOWER MENTAL BODY
(CONCRETE THOUGHT)
INTELLECT

5th CHAKRA
3rd CHAKRA
2nd CHAKRA

7th PRINCIPLE
PHYSICAL BODY
+
ETHERIC BODY
OR
ETHERIC DOUBLE

ACTIVITY

FOOD + O2

6th PRINCIPLE
EMOTIONAL BODY
OR
ASTRAL BODY

ATOMIC MATTER

LOW VIBRATIONAL BODIES

CHAPTER I

OVERVIEW OF THE STATIONS IN HUMAN DEVELOPMENT

During one life span, human beings traverse existence going through different and progressive cycles of seven year periods. From birth to age seven, an individual's life is tinted with the characteristics and energies of the First or Root Chakra which, during this fragment of time, becomes the outstanding influence and determinant force shaping the experiences and development of the person at that stage. In point of fact, issues related to this chakra appear as the basic trend in the life of a person for the first seven years of planetary existence.

In addition, the entire larger period of seven years is fragmented in smaller cycles of one year duration. Each of these little cycles is under the predominant influence of one of the seven major central chakras, starting out with the First or Root Chakra and progressing in ascendant manner. In this way, a human being lives the first year of life under the main double influence of the First or Root Chakra energy; the second year of life under the main energies of the First or Root Chakra (corresponding to the larger cycle of seven years) as well as the Second or Sacral Chakra (corresponding to the second smaller cycle of one year). The third year of life will then be influenced by the energies of the First or Root Chakra and the   ; the fourth year of life will be under the energies of the First or Root Chakra and the Fourth or Heart Chakra and so on until the completion of the seven year cycle.

The second large cycle of seven years (ages eight to fourteen), goes on under the main influence of the Second or Sacral Chakra in general plus the secondary influences of each chakra corresponding to each smaller fragment of one year duration. When seven large cycles of seven years each have passed (age 49), at age 50, a new round of cycles commence, again under the influence of the First or Root Chakra energy and proceeds once more in ascendant fashion. Only that this time lessons and opportunities for growth appear at a higher octave of evolution.

Even prior to the birth time human beings undergo these various chakra energy phases while existing in the mother's womb. Although in this circumstance the cycles of development elapse in an inverted order: They start at the level of the Seventh or Crown Chakra and end with the development of the First or Root Chakra which will connect the baby to the external world at the time of birth.(See table #1)

On the road of transformation, as lessons are learned and challenges faced and overcome, spiritual growth takes place and the human being becomes progressively ready to open up to receive and brace within its bodies or vehicles the higher vibratory energies of higher consciousness that would allow him/her access to new, more expanded realities. So it becomes the most important task for human beings taking care of the purification of their material constitution (lower bodies) in order to be able to offer Spirit the most favorable conditions and the outmost refined vehicles for its full manifestation on the physical plane.

At each ascending station, the individual counts with renewed energy and enlarged states of consciousness to continue growing through new and different challenges and learning experiences in life. It is important at this point to make a parallel between the individual human being and humanity as a whole, since in the same manner as individuals progressively develop and grow, so does humanity at large by going through different periods of development as well.

TABLE #1

Large Cycles	Small Cycles						
Birth - 7y/o Root Ch.	Age 1 +1st Ch.	Age 2 +2nd Ch.	Age 3 +3rd Ch.	Age 4 +4th Ch.	Age 5 +5th Ch.	Age 6 +6th Ch.	Age 7 +7th Ch.
8 - 14 y/o Sacral Ch.	Age 8 +1st Ch.	Age 9 +2nd Ch.	Age 10 +3rd Ch.	Age 11 +4th Ch.	Age 12 +5th Ch.	Age 13 +6th Ch.	Age 14 +7th Ch.
15 - 21 y/o Solar P. Ch.	Age 15 +1st Ch.	Age 16 +2nd Ch.	Age 17 +3rd Ch.	Age 18 +4th Ch.	Age 19 +5th Ch.	Age 20 +6th Ch.	Age 21 +7th Ch.
22 - 28 y/o Heart Ch.	Age 22 +1st Ch.	Age 23 +2nd Ch.	Age 24 +3rd Ch.	Age 25 +4th Ch.	Age 26 +5th Ch.	Age 27 +6th Ch.	Age 28 +7th Ch.
29 - 35 y/o Throat Ch.	Age 29 +1st Ch.	Age 30 +2nd Ch.	Age 31 +3rd Ch.	Age 32 +4th Ch.	Age 33 +5th Ch.	Age 34 +6th Ch.	Age 35 +7th Ch.
36 - 42 y/o 3rd Eye Ch.	Age 36 +1st Ch.	Age 37 +2nd Ch.	Age 38 +3rd Ch.	Age 39 +4th Ch.	Age 40 +5th Ch.	Age 41 +6th Ch.	Age 42 +7th Ch
43 - 49 y/o Crown Ch.	Age 43 +1st Ch.	Age 44 +2nd Ch.	Age 45 +3rd Ch.	Age 46 +4th Ch.	Age 47 +5th Ch.	Age 48 +6th Ch.	Age 49 +7th Ch.

HIGHER OCTAVE ENERGY FREQUENCIES

Large Cycles	Small Cycles						
50 - 56 y/o Root Ch.	Age 50 +1st Ch.	Age 51 +2nd Ch.	Age 52 +3rd Ch.	Age 53 +4th Ch.	Age 54 +5th Ch.	Age 55 +6th Ch.	Age 56 +7th Ch.
57 - 63 y/o Sacral Ch.	Age 57 +1st Ch.	Age 58 +2nd Ch.	Age 59 +3rd Ch.	Age 60 +4th Ch.	Age 61 +5th Ch.	Age 62 +6th Ch.	Age 63 +7th Ch.
64 - 70 y/o Solar P. Ch.	Age 64 +1st Ch.	Age 65 +2nd Ch.	Age 66 +3rd Ch.	Age 67 +4th Ch.	Age 68 +5th Ch.	Age 69 +6th Ch.	Age 70 +7th Ch.
71 - 77 y/o Heart Ch.	Age 71 +1st Ch.	Age 72 +2nd Ch.	Age 73 +3rd Ch.	Age 74 +4th Ch.	Age 75 +5th Ch.	Age 76 +6th Ch.	Age 77 +7th Ch.
78 - 84 y/o Throat Ch.	Age 78 +1st Ch.	Age 79 +2nd Ch.	Age 80 +3rd Ch.	Age 81 +4th Ch.	Age 82 +5th Ch.	Age 83 +6th Ch.	Age 84 +7th Ch.
85 - 91 y/o 3rd Eye Ch.	Age 85 +1st Ch.	Age 86 +2nd Ch.	Age 87 +3rd Ch.	Age 88 +4th Ch.	Age 89 +5th Ch.	Age 90 +6th Ch.	Age 91 +7th Ch.
92 - 98 y/o Crown Ch.	Age 92 +1st Ch.	Age 93 +2nd Ch.	Age 94 +3rd Ch.	Age 95 +4th Ch.	Age 96 +5th Ch.	Age 97 +6th Ch.	Age 98 +7th Ch.

Baby Period

The human baby undergoes the process of awakening, step by step, to the physical world and becoming adapted to a new situation of restrictions and limitations within a physical body. A baby, for the most part, sleeps while the physical body is being built upon and the soul frequently moves in and out of it, allowing the infant to still possess some kind of consciousness of the inner or spiritual world.

The Seventh or Crown Chakra of a baby is quite open while the First or Root Chakra is somewhat closed. Therefore the soul must labor and struggle in the task of opening it, since this chakra is the means of connecting to Earth and grounding into the physical plane of existence.

The electromagnetic field or aura of a baby is completely open as it is underdeveloped, making the child extremely exposed and impressionable. Hence, a baby is very vulnerable to influences from its surrounding environment. The only protection from external forces for a baby is provided by the parents' electromagnetic fields, especially the mother's since even posterior to birth a pronounced energy connection exists between mother and child throughout their entire life spans.

Of tremendous importance during this period of development is to provide the baby with breast feeding, for this is the means of administering not only physical aliment but also pranic energy through small secondary chakras located at the nipples of the mother.

Early Childhood Period

This period marks the beginning of development for the Second or Sacral Chakra, bringing the child in touch with different emotions and also, for the first time, with the feeling of being separated from the mother or the sense of being an individual person.

Children usually live in a fantasy world of their own and at this stage they project their energy toward all those external objects of their liking and which become parts of their being. The child acts more open toward others and begins to learn how to relate to them through a primary kind of love.

By the age of seven an energetic shield has formed at the opening of each chakra, thus protecting the child from external incoming influences and making it feel safe. During this period the most active is the etheric body of the person, which is mainly in charge of the growth of the physical body at this particular stage when the etheric energy can easily work on the purification of the physical body without much interference from the expression of the emotional body.

Intermediate Period Between Age Seven and Adolescence

During this period, the development of the   commences with the opening of new mental abilities. Often, mental energy is used by children in order to heighten their fantasy lives. By observing children at play we may discover deep spiritual aspirations and goals they came to fulfill during the present life, since these usually surface in their games while they are unconsciously expressing certain qualities.

Adolescent Period

This is a period frequently chaotic, characterized by physical/emotional shifts and confusion. The energy centers or chakras are often totally out of balance. It is the beginning of the Fourth or Heart Chakra development which brings about the emergence of new levels of emotion. Sexuality and romantic love arise, friends become extremely important in the life of the individual, the emotional reality changes drastically, and new desires as well as vulnerabilities become apparent.

At this stage the person is desperately seeking a true identity and struggling between its own ideas about the self and who she/he must be to others. Obviously this produces a tremendous mental tension and burden on the person. During this period of development the astral body of the individual, which is the depositary of all feelings and emotions, becomes more active, thus giving way to the appearance of passionate expressions that involve sexuality as well as aggressive behavior. This produces, as a consequence, impurities that begin to form obstructions at the level of the energy or etheric body.

Adult Period

This is the period when the mental body of the individual becomes more defined and developed. Usually the person is now ready to settle down with a job to provide for self and family. Also the capacity for loving expands to reach the personal family. If the Fourth or Heart Chakra is further developed, this loving capacity can extend even farther to include larger groups such as coworkers, sport mates, or humanity in general.

This phase regularly marks the beginning of development for the Fifth or Throat Chakra which expands the possibilities for self expression and learning to give as well as to receive. If the Sixth or Third Eye Chakra also grows in development, the individual faces opportunities to discover the essential oneness of all things and the tremendous value of each part within the whole of existence.

Maturity Period

This is the time for the Seventh or Crown Chakra to develop and for the   to become more balanced. As the person advances toward old age and eventual death, he/she should be able to process higher rates of energy and thus the focus of its attention drifts from purely material, mundane existence toward a more spiritual one. The individual at this stage commonly develops a deeper personal relationship with Divinity which conduces to a serene and loving state of existence.

It is important to point out that all these stages in the development of a human being during one life period do not occur necessarily in a fixed order for the emotional, mental and spiritual aspects, since superposition is always present and the growth process is different for each individual, depending on the degree of spiritual awareness, personal strengths and weaknesses, different challenges to face, and willingness to learn and work on the path of advancement.

Taking into account a deeper and broader knowledge, we may say that each of these phases is tinted with the characteristics that emerge from the predominant effect of one of the Cosmic Rays that constitute the person's make up. These rays are: the physical body ray, the emotional body ray, the mental body ray, the integrated personality ray, the soul ray and the monad ray.

While going through the first stages of physical life, that is, during infancy, a predominant influence is felt from the "physical body ray" of the person. This manifests mainly as the imperative need to satisfy purely the physical body's necessities, outside the domain of any mental discernment or emotional aspiration.

As the phases of growth progress a gradual shift occurs, from the directive of the physical body ray to that of the "emotional body ray." The child now becomes more focused on the emotional body and starts experiencing certain appetites beyond the purely physical wanting. The lower intellectual mind however is not yet sufficiently developed.

Later on a new displacement ensues, from the command of the emotional body ray to the dominium of the "mental body ray." Now adolescents and young adults begin to move their focus toward their lower mental bodies. The necessity to know more, inquire and explore arises; thus intellectual growth advances. Young adults start having certain ambitions and work toward the end of achieving them, as well as achieving power of any kind. Generally speaking, their conduct fluctuates between sensual, emotional and mental.

Approximately at middle age an adult individual should manage the way to somehow harmonize the functioning of its three lower natures: physical, emotional and lower mental. And this happens under the direction of the "personality ray'" energy. The behavior of the person now results in a more blended manner of manifestation. As the capacity for thinking and reasoning continue developing, the individual procures to himself increasing capability to influence and direct others. Special care must be implemented in order to not misuse these growing capacities toward selfish ends. Nevertheless, at this point in evolution, the person is mainly focused on its "ego personality" which has a general divisive tendency resulting in separatist and self-satisfying behavior.

The human being, sooner or later, progresses in the direction of the spiritual journey, expanding the ability of refined perception and maximizing involvement with the soul in order to receive its guidance. At this time, more harmonious coordination among the functioning of the three lower bodies occur, demonstrating a certain degree of integration of these bodies. This unification makes possible the appearance and now prevalent control of the individual's "personality ray," which represents the blended energies of the three lower bodies working conjointly. Also, at this level the influence of the "soul ray" can be faintly perceived.

Then along the path of consciousness awakening, the individual becomes more sensitive to the needs of others, starts losing selfishness gradually and develops extended love for others that do not belong to its personal circles such as family, friends, work, religion, country or race. This is the awakening of a larger consciousness that we call "group consciousness." Now the necessity to help others becomes noticeable and denotes the gradually increasing command and inevitable emergence of the individual's "soul ray," which eventually must take over fully and exert control of all the personality expressions of the person. The whole process may be viewed as a gradual surrendering of the individual to the lead of the soul ray that always works on a foundation of love and unity.

These stations of human development are reiterated during the course of each new life period or reincarnation of the person. The individual soul extension carries the potentiality of evolving the entirety of all plausible human monadic endowments and does so through experiencing innumerable planetary incarnations under the guidance of different cosmic rays until the goal of mastering all ray's energies is achieved and perfectly shown while still being within a physical body. This consists in manifesting on Earth, or bringing from latency to activity the three divine aspects as follows: Will/Power/Purpose of God – Love/Wisdom of God – Active Intelligence of God.

The highest manifestation of the first God's aspect or Will/Power/Purpose while incarnated in a human physical body is to manifest the will for good toward everything in creation. The highest demonstration of the second God's aspect or Love/Wisdom is to exhibit the highest form of love by addressing only to the divine spark (monad) in each human being (seeing everybody as pure spirit), as well as encompassing within the heart the entire creation. Finally, the highest manifestation of the third God's aspect or Active Intelligence is to demonstrate a transparent, pure mind and impeccable actions.

When the person becomes really cognizant of these proceedings, the desire to cooperate consciously with this otherwise inevitable natural process arises and is felt in different degrees of intensity. In this manner, the course of individual human transformation or spiritual metamorphosis can be sped up considerably, although most likely many, many planetary reincarnations will be necessary in order to accomplish these stages of evolution and awakening of consciousness.

In summary: Human development and evolution takes place externally in the bodies of manifestation, as much as internally as a gradual awakening of consciousness. It is an automatic, unavoidable process that is accomplished through the journeys of the individual soul extension and conscious, aware cooperation with this process accelerates it, thus bringing us closer to the ultimate spiritual goal. In addition, our thoughts, mental attitude and actions have the power of either support or hinder this natural process.

This evolutionary process takes the human being from a state of fragmentation and separation toward a state of wholeness; from the termination of the "small self" to the rebirth of the "bigger Self" and furthermore, as a microcosm the human being echoes, in a smaller scale, the entire evolution of the cosmos.

Several "Small Journeys" Become our "Major Journey"

During each period of human planetary life or reincarnation or "small journey," the human being undergoes transformation at all levels; physical, emotional, mental and spiritual. He/she goes through an innate process of evolution during the span of time encompassed between conception and death. Such a process goes on uninterrupted in progressive phases that take place both in a conscious or an unconscious manner, no matter what the circumstances may be.

Each time the individual returns to planet Earth for one of the "minor journeys" he/she becomes submerged into a heavy and deep sleep, an illusory state of reality where we forget our wholeness and then must work to learn something with a purpose, until awakening takes us back to the veritable reality of our existence which is the spiritual reality where we manifest as pure consciousness, intelligence and love.

During the period of being "asleep" and "forgetful," we identify ourselves solely with the individualized "I" or ego part of our personality which perceives itself as an isolated fragment and consequently experiences fear and a sense of vulnerability, especially knowing that death will claim it someday. Simultaneously, this separated fragment works desperately to aggrandize and inflate itself with the purpose of having a sense of security as well as the fulfillment of its desires.

Even if there is a purpose for coming on these journeys, we must always try to keep present in mind that this is not our ultimate reality. This is temporary and we must not allow ourselves to be seduced and trapped by this illusion and the superficial appearance of things. Appearances are only useful for us to learn how to go beyond them, to see further and rediscover the true reality of spirit.

Planetary life can be compared to a theatrical play where we are actors and the public at unison. We must learn to observe, to witness without seriously identifying ourselves with any of the roles we play, since our true higher being remains above the ups and downs we experience here on Earth through our ego/personality. We are here each time to know more and more about matter, to transform matter and to awaken from the state of sleep and dream. Thus we will move from states of ordinary consciousness to those of expanded superconsciousness.

Looking at the larger picture we may see that evolution continues after each physical death during the intermissions on the spiritual worlds, during innumerable planetary reincarnations and infinitely on a cosmic path of ascension. This is our "major journey." On this spiritual road of transformation, human beings pass through what we call "initiations" which represent introductions to new, more aware and expanded levels of consciousness that mark increasing degrees of integration within the individual.

SYNTHESIS

<u>Stations in Human Development</u>

- During one life span human beings go through cycles of seven years, each influenced by the energy of the chakras or energy centers, commencing with the First or Root Chakra for the first seven years of life and progressing in ascending manner every seven year periods.
- Each period of seven years is also divided in smaller cycles of one year which are as well under the influence of the seven major chakras in an ascending manner.
- At age 50, a new round of seven year cycles start, but at a higher octave of evolution.
- On the road of transformation (purification of the lower bodies), challenges are faced and lessons learned, leading to the necessary spiritual growth.
- As the individual progresses through stages of evolution and growth, so does humanity as a whole.
- During the baby period the soul works on the opening of the First or Root Chakra. The person must awaken step by step to existence in a physical world.
- The early childhood period marks the beginning of development for the Second or Sacral Chakra.
- The intermediate period (ages seven to fourteen) marks the commencement of the opening of the
- The adolescence period is the beginning of the Fourth or Heart Chakra development.
- The adult period marks further development of the Fourth or Heart Chakra and the beginning of development for the Fifth or Throat Chakra and the Sixth or Brow Chakra.
- The maturity period starts the development of the Seventh or Crown Chakra and the balance of the
- Each phase of development in a human being is influenced by the energies of the cosmic rays of his/her constitution as follows: Physical body ray, emotional body ray, mental body ray, personality ray and soul ray.
- The stations of human development are repeated during each new life or reincarnation (small journeys) until the individual reaches the goal of manifesting, while in a physical planetary existence, the highest expressions of the three divine aspects: Ray I of Will/Power/Purpose of God, Ray II of Love/Wisdom of God and Ray III of Active Intelligence of God (major journey).
- Human evolution happens at both external level (in the bodies of manifestation) and internal level (awakening of consciousness).
- Conscious cooperation and work accelerates the natural process.
- Our thoughts, mental attitude and actions can either support or hinder this process.
- As a microcosm the human being echoes the entire evolution of the macrocosm.

CHAPTER II

STATES OF CONSCIOUSNESS

In human beings, "pure consciousness" or "pure awareness" (infinite spirit) functions at different levels and with different degrees of awareness throughout their vehicles of manifestation that allow them to go through planetary human evolution which takes place at the lower worlds of existence, namely the physical, emotional (astral) and lower mental planes of manifestation.

Individuals constantly move among three different states of consciousness while incarnated in a physical body:

- <u>Deep sleep</u>, when the physical senses are completely inactive, the degree of awareness may be extremely faint and there is minimal capacity for perception.
- <u>Sleep with dreaming</u>, when the person can perceive, think and experience, although not through the physical senses but through the 'astral senses." In this situation, the state of consciousness is somewhat more alert.
- <u>Awake state</u> (self-consciousness), when the individual experiences daily life with full activity of the physical senses, emotions and intellectual capacity.

As the human being progresses on the spiritual road of evolution, it becomes progressively ready to uncover or awaken to the existence of higher and broader states of consciousness with increasing degrees of awareness as well. Thus, the individual discovers the following levels:

- <u>Soul consciousness</u>, when the person becomes aware of his/her existence as a soul extension, beyond the physical body. Therefore he/she connects with the soul. At the same time the individual recognizes the same in others and discovers points of deep connection with all human beings (group consciousness).
- <u>Cosmic consciousness</u>, when the person realizes himself/herself as essential spirit that is part of a vast, infinite spirit and can detachedly observe the activity of his/her personality without identifying with it. This state of consciousness brings about the manifestation of enormous creativity, intuitive ability and wisdom. Our spirit melds with the spirit in everything else and absolute trust develops.
- <u>Divine or God consciousness</u>, when the individual feels and knows the presence of God in all creation. The awareness of interconnection among all forms and beings in creation is complete.
- <u>Total oneness consciousness</u>, when the person spontaneously merges entirely with all (God), feeling the wholeness as itself.

This last state of consciousness is the final goal of returning to the pristine condition of "pure consciousness," "pure awareness," "infinite spirit" or God. Eventually we should achieve this clear state of non-duality. The entry portal to our permanent and eternal state of union with the Source of everything is meditation, and through it we shall keep this connection unobstructed.

A human being on the process of evolution (ascending arc) undergoes certain transformation that involve the evolution of form (which is the evolution of the different bodies of manifestation), as well as a parallel expansion of consciousness or awakening to the higher states of it.

These entire proceedings take place during several planetary life times or incarnations and the main purpose of it is to experience material conditions, recognizing matter also as a manifestation of spirit and finally attaining liberation from enslavement within dense matter and from the tyranny of the ego functioning through the lower or conceptual mind. In order to do this we must rediscover higher, expanded and enlightened states of consciousness that function outside time/space limitations.

The first step to be able to move in this direction is to discover ourselves as spirit that is witnessing everything as an unbiased observer and not a body. In this manner and progressing further, the sense of duality and separation vanishes and the person knows itself as a part of an inseparable whole. Thus we recognize all forms within creation, including ourselves and others without exceptions as being atoms that constitute the entirety of God's body of manifestation.

The individual now is capable of living in a sustained and intense state of being absolutely conscious in the now or present moment. For such a person, there is no longer "linear time" but "circular time" (eternity). A person becomes capable of living in this state of "eternal present" when its consciousness/awareness enlarges sufficiently to encompass all the levels of mind, retracing them to its foundation. Yet further, the individual is able to perceive the presence of God in every existing thing and knows, without a doubt, this is the only original fountain and river of life. Ultimately the expansion progresses to melding with and becoming one with the entirety of creation (the external as much as the internal, subtle worlds of existence) and non-creation (the "void" or state of ultimate nothingness with infinite possibilities of future energy/forms).

All these states of consciousness formerly described exist within us and within the whole creation now.

DIAGRAM #2
Ideal Expansion of a Human Being's Desires and Love

Love for the entire creation

↑

Love for the whole humanity

↑

Love for a whole country

↑

Love for a group in the community (sports – job – church)

↑

Love for a partner, family and friends

↑

Selfish desires and love for oneself (me first)

DIAGRAM #3
Creation, Manifestation, Evolution

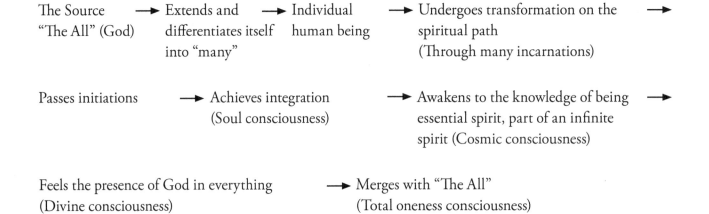

The Source → Extends and → Individual → Undergoes transformation on the →
"The All" (God)   differentiates itself   human being   spiritual path
into "many"   (Through many incarnations)

Passes initiations → Achieves integration → Awakens to the knowledge of being →
(Soul consciousness)   essential spirit, part of an infinite
spirit (Cosmic consciousness)

Feels the presence of God in everything → Merges with "The All"
(Divine consciousness)   (Total oneness consciousness)

DIAGRAM #4
The Individual Human Being's Spiritual Journey

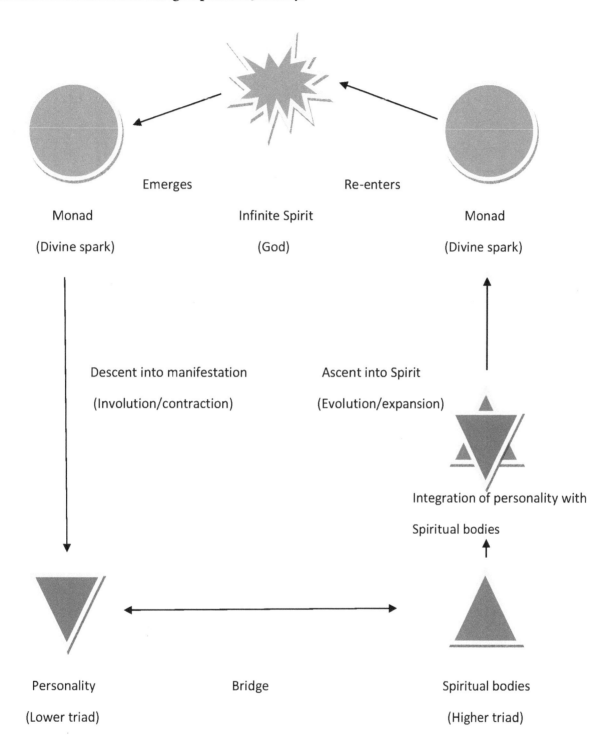

Emerges		Re-enters
Monad	Infinite Spirit	Monad
(Divine spark)	(God)	(Divine spark)

Descent into manifestation

(Involution/contraction)

Ascent into Spirit

(Evolution/expansion)

Integration of personality with

Spiritual bodies

Personality	Bridge	Spiritual bodies
(Lower triad)		(Higher triad)

SYNTHESIS

- Human beings develop and grow externally as well as internally through seven year cycles, each under the influence of chakra energies, starting from the first (Root chakra) to the seventh (Crown chakra).
- Each large cycle of seven years is divided in seven one year periods under the secondary influence of the chakra energies, also in ascending order.

- At age 50, after seven large cycles are completed, a new round of cycles commence, but this time, under a higher octave of chakra energies.
- Human beings undergo transformation through a process of growth by learning lessons and facing challenges which are conducive to evolution of form (external) and the awakening and expansion of consciousness (internal).
- Babies must awaken and adapt to the restrictions and limitations of being in a body in the physical world. The soul moves in and out of it. The fist chakra (Root chakra) must be opened in order to connect with and ground into Earth. The electromagnetic field of a baby is yet undeveloped and open, thus making the child very vulnerable to influences from the surrounding environment.
- During early childhood the second chakra (Sacral chakra) begins to develop. The child comes in touch with different emotions, begins to realize it is separated from its mother, and he/she becomes more open to other human beings.
- During the intermediate period (age seven to adolescence) the develops. Mental activity increases.
- During adolescence, the fourth chakra (Heart chakra) begins to develop and new levels of emotions, romantic love and sexuality appear more predominantly.
- During the adult period the fifth (Throat chakra) and the sixth chakra (Brow chakra) start to develop, thus expanding the possibilities for self-expression and perception of unity.
- The maturity period brings opportunities for developing the seventh chakra (Crown chakra) and balancing the   . Now the focus of attention becomes mostly spiritual.
- The energy of the "physical body ray" of a person predominates during early infancy and manifests mainly as the need to satisfy necessities of the physical body.
- Later on the "emotional body ray" takes over and its energy predominates.
- Then starts the predominant command of the "mental body ray" which produces a shift of attention toward the lower mental body in adolescents and young adults.
- Under the energy of the "personality ray," a middle age adult is steered toward blending and harmonizing the functioning of its three lower natures (physical – emotional – lower mental).
- When the energy of the "soul ray" emerges as predominant, the individual gradually loses selfishness, becomes more sensitive to the needs of others, and feels the need to provide service to others.
- These stations of human development (under seven ray's influence) are repeated during each incarnation until the individual masters the energies of all rays of creation.
- Conscious cooperation in the natural process of evolution contributes to accelerate it.
- This process takes the human being from a state of separation to a state of wholeness.
- In human beings "pure consciousness," or "pure awareness," or "infinite spirit" functions at different levels and with different degrees of awareness.
- The states of consciousness are: Deep sleep state – Sleep with dreams state – Awake state (self-consciousness) – Soul consciousness state – Cosmic consciousness state – Divine consciousness state – Total oneness consciousness state.
- Our spiritual growth, through several planetary incarnations, conduce us toward the higher states of consciousness.

CHAPTER III

CONSCIOUS WORK ON THE SPIRITUAL ROAD

<u>Overview</u>

Our conscious spiritual work must be directed toward the following points, with the purpose of accelerating our growth and the manifestation of our full human potential:

1. <u>Learning metaphysics (beyond the physical) and allowing spirituality to surface</u>
    This knowledge will bring us out of ignorance about our real constitution, the nature of the cosmos and its laws, the process of evolution and our place/purpose within the universal web of cosmic design.
2. <u>Self-observation and analysis (introspection)</u>
    This scrutiny must be carried on carefully as well as in a detached manner. It implies to have the courage to face the activities of our personality and should be done at all levels: physical, emotional, mental and spiritual. We are called to observe our actions, habits, attitude, reactions, feelings, motives, intentions and aspirations. As aids in this process we may use the information from our personal astrology chart, numerology chart and our personal cosmic ray makeup analysis. These can show us which are the forces working through our constitution and make clearer to us what are our weaknesses as well as our strengths, which are the tools we possess to do our spiritual work.
3. <u>Reaching an accurate conclusion about our present selves</u>
    This is the result of the former evaluation of self, if it was done with total honesty, fearlessness and clarity of mind.
4. <u>Self-correction and the beginning of transformation</u>
    This shall be done also at all levels (physical, emotional, mental and spiritual), and requires a strong determination to work on ourselves in order to build a firm moral character with positive thought patterns. It involves terminating deleterious habits as well as changing attitudes and false perception of reality. In addition, blocks and leaks of vital energy in our chakra system should be eliminated and our strengths must be used for the benefit of transforming our weaknesses into something positive and vanishing our fears.
5. <u>Remembering always that we are not alone in this venture</u>
    Guidance is ever available through different means and we may ask for help at any moment of our life. The help may come from more advanced persons and spiritual teachers in the flesh, from guides and teachers in spirit, and from our own higher self. If we are deeply connected to the cosmos as a whole, help will always come to us in one way or another. We must learn to become sensitive and aware enough to receive and understand messages from the inner worlds, which are destined to orient us on our evolutionary journey.

6. <u>Developing the practice of spiritual disciplines</u>
   This will help us to remain in awareness of our links with higher levels of existence. Spiritual disciplines may include:
   - <u>The practice of prayer and meditation</u>: These open doors of access to the spiritual inner planes and help us to be more conscious of the presence of God within ourselves and the entirety of creation. As well, the different layers of our personality can be gradually cleansed and veils that obscure the truth can be lifted.
   - <u>The practice of dream work</u>: This will connect us with the inner planes as well and help us in the process of self-discovery and knowledge.
   - <u>The practice of Yoga and different energy exercises (Chi Gong – Tai Chi Chuan)</u>: Through these, the ability for concentration is developed, the energy centers or chakras are opened and activated and finally these make it possible to more readily align body, mind and spirit.

7. <u>Bringing all that has been learned to a level of concrete practice</u>
   This means that we must incorporate and demonstrate all our learning in our daily lives, in a practical manner.

8. <u>Practicing service for others</u>
   This is really a demonstration of care and love for others, humanity in general and all the kingdoms of nature.

Thus our spiritual work little by little takes us to establish conscious connections between the material world and the subtle worlds of spirit; to acknowledge that we are in reality multidimensional beings functioning in unison at different levels of existence and also to acknowledge that spirit has power over matter. In this manner, our work results in the development of close and true relationships of self with God, with our higher Self, with the invisible spiritual worlds, with other humans, with the other kingdoms of nature and with the whole cosmos.

<u>Results Obtained Through Our Conscious Spiritual Labor</u>
<u>At Physical External Level</u>

- Correct breathing.
- Correct diet and manner of eating.
- Perfect balance between activity, rest and sleeping times.
- Appropriate exercises.
- Correct expenditure and recharging of energy.
- Appropriate sexual activity.
- Evolution of the physical body to become a vehicle which is more apt for the soul extension.
- Full and deep enjoyment of nature.
- Correct actions that are rather born from a main focus of attention in the soul extension. This involves:
  - Command over speech (demonstrating the right use of speech by using words that transmit affection, positive criticism if needed, support, inspiration, justice and truth), silence (not responding to lower vibrations and allowing communion with Self and God), and deeds (demonstration of honesty overall).
  - Attitude of sharing and cooperation in any relationship with others.
  - Heightened creativity and problem solving capacity.

- Attitude of respect for nature and all life (demonstration of harmlessness and non violence).
- Service to help others without conditions of return or payment.
- Purity of life by demonstrating humility, compassion, honesty, respect and wisdom.
- Redirection of focus toward collective rather than individual works.

At Emotional and Mental External Levels

- State of dispassion or non reaction in the face of either pleasure or suffering (abiding unperturbed at the center of being).
- State of detachment (not indifference), or perfectly knowing that all manifested things are only temporary.
- State of inclusive love or unity. That is, existing beyond the boundaries of inflexible structures such as races, cultures, countries, religions, institutions and even families.
- Correct discrimination or choice by using properly the lower mind in order to discern the false from the authentic and be able to select that which advances us on the spiritual path.
- Annihilation of egotism, arrogance, pride, competition, criticism, judgment, violence, confrontation, defensiveness, all fears, doubt and isolation.
- Expression of equilibrium, humility, gentleness, certitude, focus, forbearance, patience, open-mindedness, gaiety and love.
- Enhanced capacity for the perception of spiritual forces within all substance and forms, which results in remarkable changes in our reality perception. The ability for a deeper perception, farther than superficial appearances, becomes clearly manifested.
- Heightened capacity for enjoying beauty in general, in nature as well as in artistic expressions.
- Discovery of an intense sense of responsibility toward all of creation.
- Internal purification.

The simultaneous and parallel expansion of both the higher aspects of "love" and "knowledge" produces the outcome of "wisdom" which is the manifestation of the conjunct workings of higher mind and spirit guiding the correct use of the "will" aspect toward right actions. That is those actions that are aligned with the Divine Plan for creation.

At Spiritual Internal Level

- Full activation of the energy centers or chakras and the energy channels.
- Total purification of the lower bodies that now function in harmony and synchronicity, in an integrated manner (physical, emotional and lower mental).
- Perfect knowledge of the intended use of the lower mind and the individual will power that now are guided by the love of the heart.
- Full development of the potentials of higher mind and intuition.
- Shifting of our point of identification from the personality (lower bodies) to the soul extension and eventually to the spiritual bodies (higher triad) and the Monad (spark of spirit). This implies substituting the commands of the ego for those of the Higher-Self.
- Progressive changes in consciousness (expansions) and ultimately changes in the DNA.
- State of absolute knowing the purpose of life in manifestation and God's Divine Plan.

- State of immutable faith or knowing with certainty that God's Will is one with ours.
- Absolute comprehension and accord with Divine Laws and cosmic equilibrium.
- State of complete, immovable peace, calm and clarity under any circumstance of life.
- Always staying at the center of being.
- Constant awareness of the divine presence within.
- State of transcendence of "duality" or the "pair of opposites" (balanced state of consciousness).
- Total transfiguration of the "personal individual self" into the "universal self."
- Enlightenment.

Final Results

- Planetary ascension: the transit from the fourth kingdom of nature (Human kingdom) to the fifth kingdom (Spirit kingdom) and to the Hierarchy of planet Earth.
- Cosmic ascension: transiting the roads of "higher evolution."

The entire proceeding of spiritual growth can be viewed as stages of returning to a state of pristine unity with Divinity, through gradual awakening of consciousness from self consciousness (individuation and apparent separation state) to total oneness consciousness.

Practical Guide for Doing the Spiritual Work

- Study and learn about the real constitution of human beings and their place within the larger cosmic scheme.
- Study your astrological chart.
- Study your numerology chart.
- Study and learn about your personal cosmic rays constitution.
- Study metaphysics.
- Self observation, analysis and conclusions about the self (Remembering your life from childhood to present).
- Dream work.
- Practice of meditation.
- Practice of prayers.
- Self correction and beginning the process of conscious transformation and growth.
- Face your fears and bring forth your courage.
- Read scriptures and spiritual literature.
- Remain in contact with nature, practicing contemplation of it and developing respect and reverence for it. Accustom yourself to feel as part of the body of our planet Earth and to attune to its resonance. Expand this feeling to the entire cosmos.
- Practice being totally "present" or aware at all times during your daily activities.
- Practice absolute acceptance of what is at the present moment.
- Remain aware and alert about the connection between your acts and their consequences. Thoughts and emotions drive us to act, therefore we must watch the way we think and feel.
- Maintain a proper diet and manner of eating.
- Maintain proper breathing and practice deep breathing exercises.

- Maintain proper sexual attitude and activity.
- Practice appropriate physical exercises, including energy exercises.
- Dedicate enough time to rest and sleeping.
- Allow yourself to enjoy and laugh. Connect with the natural joy of the soul.
- Dedicate time to productive work.
- Eliminate addictions at all levels.
- Encourage positive thinking and attitudes.
- Maintain proper speech and times for silence.
- Work consciously on your energy body in order to dissolve blockages, seal leaks and develop the energy centers or chakras.
- Practice absolute non-violence at all levels.
- Practice absolute honesty.
- Practice compassion and service to others.
- Use tools that can aid you in this process: colors, sounds, fragrances, massage or other types of energy therapies, hypnosis, age and past life regression, progression and time line techniques by appropriate professionals.

In summary, it is our duty and purpose here on Earth to work with total consciousness to develop a firm will to purify ourselves and open ourselves in order to receive higher vibrations from pure spirit and thus become an alive and real temple for God's manifestation.

SYNTHESIS

Our conscious spiritual work must be directed toward:

- Learning metaphysics which will conduce to self knowledge, knowledge of the cosmos and awareness of God.
- Reading spiritual texts.
- Self observation and posterior work on ourselves for correction, cleansing and growth.
- Developing spiritual practices.
- Practicing in a concrete manner all the learning.
- Living in the present moment and in contact with nature.
- Learning the value of appropriate diet, manner of eating, breathing, sexual activity, physical activity, work, speech, silence, rest, enjoyment and laughter.
- Eliminating addictions at all levels.
- Living in peace and non-violence, reverence and respect for everything; as well as in absolute honesty.
- Keeping an open and positive state of mind.
- Helping others.

Our conscious spiritual work will eventually be translated into positive results and advancement at all levels: physical, emotional/mental and spiritual.

CHAPTER IV

INTEGRATION/UNIFICATION OF THE HUMAN BEING

Our conscious spiritual work upshots into awakening of consciousness, as the product of a process of harmonious amalgamation or connection among the energies of the different human bodies or vehicles for spirit manifestation. Furthermore, we must accomplish integration of the unified bodies with the Monad (spirit spark) and render them functioning under direct monadic influence.

As the forms or bodies grow, cleanse and develop, their energies blend and harmonize allowing the awareness of higher forms of consciousness to be expressed. This task of ours takes place unconsciously at first. Then, at some point, consciously throughout all the cycles of reincarnation of the soul extension, from each birth to each death and also including intermission times (inner life between incarnations).

The beginning stage entails the consolidation of the physical/etheric unit with the astral or emotional body; then follows the concordant blending of the already synchronized physical/etheric/emotional units with the lower mental body. When this is completed and the lower bodies are entirely integrated with each other and functioning consciously with a common purpose, we may say that we have attained the state of living through a "unified personality."

The following stage is to effect the merger between the unified personality and the individual soul extension. Toward this end now, the amalgamated energy of the new personality must be directed straight to the soul extension, identify with it and fully submit to its guidance. This solid unification produces a natural attraction of energy from the spiritual bodies.

The process continues with further integration of the personality/soul unit and the spiritual bodies or higher triad. It finally culminates with unification and direct connection of the former synthesis of bodies and the human Monad (divine spark), which gives us access to planetary consciousness and beyond.

The process of building up the integration of the different human bodies or principles through energetic connections takes place in the following manner:

From the physical/etheric bodies ————————————————➤ to the astral or emotional body
connection through the energy of
the

A beam of energy now projects from the   toward the soul extension and this happens as the result of the person getting focused on higher aspirations and trying to achieve them.

From the physical/etheric/ astral unit ————————————————➤ to the lower mental body
connection through the energy
of the Brow (Third Eye) chakra

Another beam of energy projects from the Brow chakra toward the soul extension, by action of the personal will.

From the three lower aspects joined together ———————————————▶ to the soul extension
           (personality)   connection through the
                                  energy of the Heart chakra

A third beam of energy projects from the Heart chakra toward the soul extension.

From the personality and soul joined together ———————————————▶ to the spiritual bodies
                                 connection of energy   (expression of the Monad)

This time, a triple beam of energy is directed from the spiritual triad toward the soul and personality which becomes thus stimulated to develop further the energetic bridge (Antahkarana) between the lower and higher minds. In this way, open and direct communication with the higher monadic level becomes possible.

Thus, our spiritual work must be focused at first on the lower bodies, with the general objective of increasing their overall vibratory frequency through purification and refinement. In this manner their energy can be translated to their elevated counterparts (spiritual triad) through the soul energy and by developing the bridge of mental substance known as "Antahkarana." Generally speaking, this work is done through:

- Purification
- Discipline
- Meditation

As the process of integration/unification of the different human principles or bodies unfold, the energies represented by the chakras ascend and consciousness awakens further.

DIAGRAM #5
MOVEMENT OF ASCENSION OF CHAKRA ENERGIES

To service for humanity   To mental and artistic creativity

6th or Third Eye Chakra   5th or Throat Chakra

1st or Root Chakra   2ond or Sacral Chakra

From personal material ambition   From physical and sexual creativity

The energy rises by transmutation

To group consciousness

4th or Heart Chakra

To focus on the soul

6th or Third Eye Chakra

5th or Throat Chakra

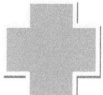

4th or Heart Chakra

From self-centered desires

From focus on the personality

The energy rises by transmutation

To focus on the spiritual triad

7th or Crown Chakra

6th or Third Eye Chakra

From focus on the soul

The energy rises and shifts

Another crucial aspect we must work on is the full awakening and concrete expression of the three divine aspects lying dormant within each one of us (the Holy Trinity). In the beginning our work is confined to the lower phases of manifestation of these divine aspects. Later on we must pay attention to their higher levels, with the main purpose of allowing them to function harmoniously in unison as one, while performing our daily activities in life.

Our task commences by bringing the focus of our attention first on the third aspect of "Active Intelligence" which is represented by the energy of the cosmic creative Ray III (Mother or Holy Spirit aspect), aiming to procure knowledge and lucid, unobstructed thinking (lower manifestation of this aspect), which eventually will shift to its corresponding elevated expression as instant knowing and guidance through intuitive comprehension. The ultimate step in this work would be to permit this third aspect of intelligence to be inundated and guided by the second divine aspect of "Love/Wisdom" which is represented by the energy of the cosmic creative Ray II (Son/Daughter aspect). Thus we must actively use the energy of disinterested love.

Lastly, we must work to uncover the higher function of the first divine aspect of "Will Power/Purpose" which is represented by the energy of the cosmic creative Ray I (Father aspect). We can do this by discovering the true purpose of our soul extension (messenger from the spiritual bodies), and the proper use of the "higher will" which acts as the transcendent leader of soul and personality.

When a human being reaches the state in which he/she is capable of fully demonstrating the higher levels of the three divine aspects, while being incarnated in a physical body, all the substance of the lower bodies (physical – astral/emotional – mental) is impregnated with intelligent light and all the actions of the personality are sensibly and wisely guided.

The ultimate purpose of us, human beings living incarnated on planet Earth, is to rediscover and remember our veritable spiritual nature, bringing to the surface all the subtle, intangible divine attributes and manifesting on Earth the splendor of the Divine.

DIAGRAM #6
TRANSMUTATION OF THE ENERGIES OF THE THREE DIVINE ASPECTS

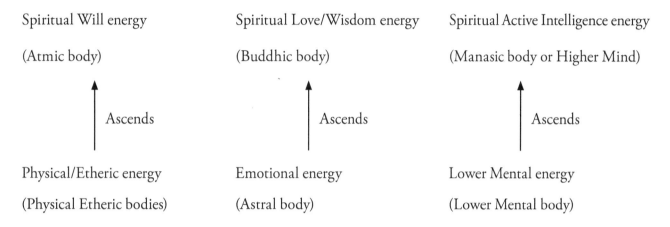

Spiritual Will energy (Atmic body) — Ascends — Physical/Etheric energy (Physical Etheric bodies)

Spiritual Love/Wisdom energy (Buddhic body) — Ascends — Emotional energy (Astral body)

Spiritual Active Intelligence energy (Manasic body or Higher Mind) — Ascends — Lower Mental energy (Lower Mental body)

Developing the energetic bridge: "Antahkarana"

This band of mental energy bridges the gap between the lower and higher mental bodies in the human constitution. It must be reinforced and developed as part of our spiritual work toward the integration/unification of our different bodies, since ultimately it will permit the elevation of the lower energies in the direction of the Monad which represents our true Self.

The bridge is expanded by means of holding a spiritual attitude in our lives in general and by remaining steadily in contact with and sensitive to the soul promptings and orientation. The entire proceeding entails practicing with a firm and focused intent on the following:

- Meditation
- Developing the faculty of intuition for guidance
- Creative imagination and visualization
- Projection techniques
- Invocation/evocation techniques
- Stabilization techniques

The practice of deep witnessing meditation per se develops the intuitive capacity of the human being and can guide us on the spiritual path.

Creative imagination can be used in the mode of visualizing a column of light, around ourselves in the place where we are standing, that connects us upward with our Monad (spirit spark) and even beyond it, as well as downward with the center of our planet Earth.

Projection techniques consist of intentionally sending a ray of light upward together with potent vibrations generated by the chanting of mantras or the chanting of any of the used names for God, through the same column of light held in our mind by means of our imagination. A few examples of what can be chanted are: "OM/AUM" – "SAT NAM" – "I AM THAT I AM." For the ray of light projected upward we may use the color of our Monadic Ray (Red, indigo, or yellow).

The invocation/evocation mechanism is simply the movement of energies that take place when we intensely desire to grow spiritually (the ascending energy of invocation). This force stimulates a responsive energy from the higher spiritual triad and Monad aspects of our constitution (the descending energy of evocation) that makes itself evident in the form of heightened intuition and guidance. The chanting of mantras also reinforces the energy of invocation.

Stabilization entails maintaining and reinforcing the newly expanded energy of the bridge through the practice of meditation and living, at all levels, a predominantly spiritual life.

In this manner, the bridge Antahkarana, step by step extends and fortifies to eventually allow the elevation of the unified and integrated human bodies or vehicles toward the Monad. This may be considered as the true resurrection of the human being.

At this point, as the outcome of our persistent and conscious work on ourselves, all our bodies and consequently the electromagnetic field (aura) they emanate, expand and enlarge tremendously, thus transforming us into vibrant, luminous beings with auras of vivid, clear colors that are patterned in beautiful geometrical forms. Now, as integrated beings, we can function equally and with full awareness at multi dimensional levels in a state of continuity of consciousness and complete cognition of our life purpose while incarnated.

Thus, the course of integration/unification takes us from self-consciousness to soul-consciousness to cosmic-consciousness to God or Divine- consciousness and finally to total unity-consciousness. And we say again that integration/unification in a human being is the outcome achieved through the arduous work done during many incarnation periods, between incarnations (within the inner worlds), and even beyond incarnations. The first target in this work is to attain the integration of the three lower bodies or personality and become a purified conduit for the activity of the soul extension.

All of us human beings, sooner or later during a given life time, will experience the feeling that impulses us with increasing intensity to investigate more; to know more about ourselves, our relations and the entire cosmos. This feeling becomes almost a compulsion that slowly opens us to become receptive to pay heed to the "voice of our soul," even faintly at first, until we render ourselves totally conscious and aware of it. In order to perceive our soul we ought to slow down and become very quiet, going deeply within.

In the beginning, we realize that we are the protagonists of a tremendous struggle between our personality which resists changes and our soul extension which impulses us toward the spiritual journey. However, eventually we shall consciously cooperate for the achievement of spiritual growth.

Up to this point, our life in general has revolved around the purpose of fulfilling our personal necessities and ambitions, such as attention to our physical body, emotional needs, studies, career, work, close friends and family. But now, the more conscious we become on the spiritual path, the more sensitive to the needs of others and respectful of all beings in nature we are.

An alignment between thoughts and feelings occurs during the proceedings of integration in the human being, in such a way that when it happens we start to "know" and "feel" always from our heart center. Also, this process takes us through the task of discerning between the things in our life that we want to conserve because they contribute to our advancement, and the ones we must wear away, simply because we no longer need them. The latter certainly includes old, rigid and deleterious habit patterns.

Integration/unification requires that we open ourselves in trust and surrender, allowing the natural process to unfold and flow freely in total accordance with divine plan that moves through us. We must understand, without any doubts, that we are all ingredients of a shared design with a single purpose: conquering the lower nature and merging with the higher toward a splendorous state of consciousness that will manifest as light, strength, peace, joy and glory.

When working on this process of integration while living material lives, under no circumstance should we reject matter, since it is absolutely necessary for the process and represents a learning field of experience. The secret lies in not confusing the means with the goal and always having present in mind the fact that the only thing that ultimately matters is within us (spirit) and the external material world is at the service of spirit and truth.

Integration/unification is then the outcome of:

- Constructing and developing our character through the purification of the lower bodies.
- Establishing contact with the soul extension and following its guidance which eventually will conduce us to establish contact with the higher spiritual bodies through the magnification of the bridge Antahkarana.
- Expressing, in daily life, impeccability of conduct and assistance to others.

SYNTHESIS

- Our conscious spiritual work leads to the complete blending of our different bodies of manifestation and the gradual awakening of our consciousness.
- In the process, strong energetic connections develop from the physical/etheric bodies to the astral/emotional body, to the soul extension and finally to the spiritual bodies (higher triad).
- The chakra energies ascend as follows:
    - From the first or Root Chakra ⟶ to the sixth or Third Eye Chakra
    - From the second or Sacral Chakra ⟶ to the fifth or Throat Chakra
    - From the ⟶ to the fourth or Heart Chakra
    - From the fourth or Heart Chakra ⟶ to the fifth or Throat Chakra ⟶ to the sixth or Third Eye Chakra
    - From the sixth or Third Eye Chakra ⟶ to the seventh or Crown Chakra
- A very important part of our spiritual work is the conscious and intentional development and strengthening of the mental bridge Antahkarana.
- A crucial aspect we must work on as well is the complete awakening, activation and expression of the three divine aspects dormant within each one of us (Holy Trinity).
- Clear discernment between what we need and what we no longer need in our lives takes place.
- Integration/unification requires us to: open up, be receptive, trust, surrender, allow and flow.
- Our sole purpose in life is to conquer our lower nature and merge with the higher one.
- Integration/unification is the outcome of working on character building, contacting the soul extension, and expressing through impeccability and service to others.

CHAPTER V

THE TRANSFORMATIVE WORK ON OURSELVES

<u>CONSTRUCTION AND DEVELOPMENT OF CHARACTER</u>

Character is built through living experiences, and certainly the social conditions of a given period carry weight on it. Character then is an addition to the foundation of temperament which comprises the entirety of the inborn characteristics of a human being.

Depending on the way we live, the character may either retrogress or progress. It deteriorates if we live mechanically in unconsciousness and ignorance; on the contrary, a strong moral character is the outcome if we live consciously and work diligently for the betterment of our condition by using the powers of thought, discernment and will properly.

Our temperament, represented by basic instincts and tendencies, has the possibility of changing for the better if we work consciously and intentionally toward improvement and building of character all through innumerable incarnation periods. This task consists in:

1 <u>Acquiring Understanding and Knowledge of our True Constitution and our Position Within the Grand Design of the Cosmos</u>

Every human being carries within, although unconsciously in most cases, a sense of duality. There is the feeling of something inside being divided, which provokes a ceaseless war between these fragments of us that manifest as the "lower self" (personality with ego identification) and the "higher self" (spiritual bodies with Divine identification). When we realize and clearly see this state, we turn more conscious and begin to desire knowing more about ourselves. This marks the beginning of learning and comprehending beyond the appearances of our very limited reality. Then, what can we do?

- We must study about our real constitution of different bodies or principles (gross and subtle), the energy system in and out of our bodies (chakras and energy channels), and the resultant electromagnetic field around us (aura).
- We ought to study all that concerns the sacred elements of nature (ether – air – fire – water – earth) and their interaction as parts of our bodies and the entire cosmos.
- We shall study about vibratory frequencies, light, colors, fragrances and sounds.
- We must instruct ourselves about true health, the real origin of what we call disease, death and reincarnation. Also, about creation, universal laws and evolution.

As the result of this investigation and studies we discover that we are not really who we think we are. We are not just a gross and dense physical body but spirit in manifestation at multidimensional levels. Then we begin to increasingly open ourselves to subtle perceptions, our unified center, our intuition which is nothing less than contact with higher levels of existence, as well as guidance from our spiritual bodies and beings of superior intelligence.

Eventually, we progress to re-learning or remembering our essential unity with all the kingdoms of nature, the whole cosmos and God, by following a process of striping away layers of illusion. The ultimate knowledge about us is the true recognition of only pure spirit as ourselves. It is also the acknowledgment of interrelatedness and interdependency among everything in existence, as well as the acceptance of equality of importance of the different roles each fragment of creation must play as parts of the whole. There are no greater or lesser positions within the cosmos; everything is spirit manifesting itself and everything is in the right place and moment.

As cells, we live within an enormous organism: the cosmos or God's body of manifestation. From this extraordinary organism we receive our life and sustenance, and when we separate our consciousness from it, we are depriving ourselves of life and support from spirit. When we do not live in complete harmony with this universal cosmic body, something becomes altered in its functioning; something turns out of equilibrium. It is our duty to contribute for its perfect balance by showing respect, love and wisdom; and by becoming totally aware of this reality.

All this knowledge and feelings undoubtedly will transport us to the next necessary steps for our healthy development and spiritual growth.

2 Self-observation and Analysis

Observation of the self must be an ongoing task, performed in a detached manner that ignores the screams of the ego, and encompassing the totality of our being at all levels: physical, emotional, mental and spiritual. In order to do this properly we must call to the fore courage, honesty, humility, clear discernment and a sense of justice.

As the result of a careful scrutiny of the self, we should be able to uncover debilities (coarse qualities) as well as strengths (more elevated qualities) in our temperament. We also discover that in reality we live with a permanent sense of duality and conflict within the self, as well as in interaction with other beings. In relation to others, we always follow the directives of separation; we create barriers, compare, judge and compete to win. Even our attitude in relation to nature, our planet, the other kingdoms (mineral – vegetal – animal), the cosmos and the Creator, is also divisive. In general, we do not feel or sense the deep spiritual/energetic connections existing all over creation. We think we are disconnected, unique, and position ourselves either above or below something.

Although in this material world of us, we are expected to learn through living in duality and dealing with different pairs of opposite, the final goal or the way out of it consists in finding the "middle way." That Is finding a nonpartisan position where we become only non judgmental observers of the duality in life, and thus we are capable of honoring each aspect equally from the understanding that we are really learning through both. This further means that we must learn to not attempt to change circumstances or persons in order to satisfy our desires.

Since cosmic energy is verily neutral in nature, the only manner to tap into it and connect with it is by maintaining a likewise neutral mental attitude of non judgment in addition to keeping a heart full of love.

Part of our discoveries is the realization that human beings in their consciousness carry the original powers of will, thought, love, choice and action. However, we must acknowledge that we should learn not to misuse these powers, nor to imprison ourselves by remaining within the ignorance of applying them in their basic forms. We must rise to the proper and exalted way of using them. Our work must be first of all observing and discovering how we are applying them to the moment in our daily living. And then attempt the necessary corrections.

In its lower application, the power of will appears as the human desire for possessions, or as certain selfish actions. In its elevated form this energy induces to higher ideals and actions. Undoubtedly, the manner in which our power of willing manifests shall affect the course of our life, other beings and even the entire cosmos.

In regard to the power of thought we must analyze carefully the way we think, and even further, what is really behind our thoughts; that is our intentions. False or corrupted intentions are those accompanied by feelings of exaggerated ambition, anger or selfishness; or those motivated by weakness, fear and pessimism. Our true and real intentions are higher and always motivated by the soul.

The manner in which we think determines our moral and mental traits. Thoughts of similar quality that are sustained consistently, end up creating habitual thought patterns that manifest automatically and affect the physical body, since the mind has supremacy over it. We must discover our thought patterns, for the nature of our thoughts mark our physical body and also exert an effect over other beings and the whole cosmos. Part of this endeavor is to observe our choices. Do they reflect the desire to advance toward spirit, or only the selfish desire to satisfy our ego?

The essence of thought is very powerful: it creates, directs and effects. These qualities of the true power of thought, in reality, belong to the higher mind, which is capable of pure thinking. When we descend to the level of the lower mind (intellect) and the level of emotions, thoughts become soiled and impure, agitated and chaotic, losing their piercing power. Our task is to elevate ourselves to the higher mental plane and in absolute silence turn one with God, before we can encounter the real power of thought.

In our self-observation process, we must include uncovering the way in which we use the power of love. In its basic form love is demanding, conditional and selfish. In its higher form it is unconditional and inclusive.

Finally, our actions represent the way we think and the choices we make, and definitely our actions produce effects on ourselves, others, the environment and the entire creation. In this way we carry on our shoulders the tremendous responsibility of constructing our own destiny (during several life periods and thereafter) and contributing to the one of others.

Thus, by scrutinizing ourselves in detail and honesty, we become fully cognizant of our temperament's characteristics or natural tendencies that we were born with. These inclinations are instinctive in nature and rooted in our past lives conduct, as much as in our biological constitution. Furthermore, along this self-observation line, unwanted and discordant attitudes and habits of our personality will be openly exposed. Such habits and attitudes are pernicious to our physical, emotional and mental health, given that they are low vibratory frequency energy conformations. Therefore, they ought to be either dissolved or transformed into energy of a higher quality. In addition, we must always remember that the harmful effects of our behavior are not solely affecting us but also has repercussions on other beings, as far as the whole of creation. The more pernicious our habits are, the denser our lower constitution becomes, impeding the flow of light and energy from the higher components of our natural makeup (soul and spiritual bodies).

As an outcome of this scrupulous observation and analysis of ourselves we are able to unearth and clearly expose our habits at all levels, our emotional reactions and mental attitudes, with both their good and defective qualities as well. Then we arrive to the point where we now have the possibility of utilizing our good qualities or strengths as tools for the work of advancing and empowering ourselves. The exposed weaknesses, of course, should be eventually transmuted into new strengths.

It is imperative that during all this process we remain very vigilant in order to be able to notice any of the ego manipulations, which will continuously attempt either to justify/minimize the weaknesses, or to aggrandize the strengths. We must avoid falling into the games of our ego and maintain enough courage and clarity to strip ourselves, looking at what we see as a reality without any distortions.

3 Attaining Accurate and Honest Conclusions About Ourselves

If we now are able to truly contemplate ourselves as we really are, without distortions or illusions, without hiding anything, we can conclude knowing in all honesty our weak as well as our strong traits. First of all we must become aware of our destructive or damaging physical habits and addictions. Then, by investigating within the domain of our thoughts and emotions, we can uncover our mental/emotional patterns which are determining our mental attitudes and emotional reactions. Thus, what we call "our personality," is composed by weak and strong points as well, in different combinations:

Weak Points	Strong Points
Gossip	Reservation/discretion
Negative criticism	Positive criticism
Prejudice	Open-mindedness
Intolerance	Tolerance
Blame	Forgiveness
Judgment/condemnation	Non-judgment/understanding
Arrogance/vanity	Humility/modesty
Desire of domination	Desire of sharing
Competition	Cooperation
Resentment	Letting go
Vindictiveness	Compassion
Envy/jealousy	Respect/acceptance
Ingratitude	Gratitude/thankfulness
Impatience/restlessness	Patience/peace
Inconstancy	Perseverance
Lying/cheating	Truthfulness/honesty
Selfishness	Generosity
Greed	Balance/contentment
Defensiveness	Non-defensiveness/calmness
Unloving	Nurturing
Cunning	Innocence
Hatred	Love
Aggressiveness/anger/violence	Gentleness
Anxiety	Calmness
Chaotic feelings and thoughts	Harmony
Regret/guilt	Freedom/peace
Worry/sorrow	Happiness/enjoyment
Withdrawal	Communication
Fear	Courage

Fear encompasses several kinds of it as follows:
- The fear of physical things such as the forces of nature and attack from persons or animals.
- The fear of non-physical things and the unknown.
- The fear of certain situations.
- The fear of judgment from others.
- The fear of disease and death.
- The fear of loneliness.
- The fear of suffering.
- The fear of failure.
- The fear of change.
- The fear of poverty.

Once we are certain about which components (weaknesses and strengths) manifest through our personality, we must also be totally aware of the present circumstances of our life. This will allow us to discover the links existing between our past actions and their present consequences (bad or good), which are shaping now the conditions in which we live.

Life behaves as a reflecting mirror constantly showing us the results of our behavior and internal workings. Thus, the external world is always reflecting back to us, according to our conduct. For instance, if we are lacking in honesty and goodness, that will be shown to us in the form of the quality of our surrounding circumstances or in the behavior of others around us. In the case that we do not realize this, either out of ignorance or because we refuse to see and accept it, something for sure will happen to shake and wake us up.

We ought to decide to fortify and support our strong components, which represent higher energy patterns, and use them to help us transmute our weak components, which represent lower energy patterns, into positive forms.

So we now have a clear picture of our present self manifesting as a personality and can more easily know the areas in which we must work to transform ourselves for the better. First of all, we should forgive ourselves with non-judgment, and only see impartially those parts that need change. We have reached the present situation in our life doing the best we knew anyway and now are more aware and knowledgeable, being better prepared to start a conscious spiritual work on ourselves. For this we must remind ourselves often of our spiritual resolve and reinforce and focus our intention on doing the work. This is the endeavor that awakens more and more the spiritual world within. When we succeed in expelling out of our being defiled desires and thoughts, then the light of spirit will inundate us, allowing true vision and knowledge.

4 Maintaining Unwavering Determination to Work on Ourselves

We must remain steadfast in our determination to work toward changing habits that are harmful for us and others as well. These changes must be effected at all levels: physical, emotional and mental. It is very important also to move out and beyond false perceptions of reality.

5 The Actual Work of Self-correction

Becoming properly informed and learning is not enough to fulfill our duty as human beings. However, it serves the purpose of satisfying our curiosity, inciting us, and further igniting the desire for change and transformation. The only way we can undergo improvement is through working on ourselves. Therefore, we should learn to take action on what we have learned and keep ever in mind that although the work we must do commences in ourselves, it will always have important positive repercussions on all components of the universe.

The first and primordial step toward self-transformation is becoming aware of those things in us that need to be changed or let go. The second step is to have the desire and be really willing to do the necessary work on releasing the patterns of negative energy within. The third step is to focus full intention on doing it.

In order to get to work, we must intentionally start to discipline ourselves. What can help guiding us and providing some kind of structure for our work is keeping in mind the following: The task of working on ourselves for spiritual advancement must be directed in general toward the attainment of transformation and elimination of internal gross qualities of energy as well as cultivation of a higher quality of energy. Our intention must be set high in order to move us in the direction of the soul extension. This will eventually imply the ending of the sense of separation from the whole of creation and God, as well as the embracing of a new sense of synthesis and unity.

The groundwork, the beginning point, is to have a distinct outline of our personality with every characteristic and tendency, as it is truly at the present time. We must know perfectly the materials and devices we possess in order to do our work. We must have discovered all the weaknesses (materials) and strengths (tools) we have. Next, it is helpful to form within the mind an exemplary model or prototype that we want to emulate and achieve as an ideal goal. Finally we must work on creating new habits for ourselves, at all levels (physical – emotional – mental – spiritual), that will not be harmful or deter us away from the spiritual path.

First of all we commence by eliminating the deleterious habits of the physical body in order to completely purify it. The physical body is the vehicle that permits the soul extension to experience within a physical plane. That is why it should be regarded as an external sanctuary for the manifestation of spirit. As such, it should be highly respected and dignified, never abused or lowered.

For us to accomplish the first stage, we must pay serious attention to our diet, the environment and manner in which we ingest aliments, the kind of physical activities engaged in (including sexual activity), the ways in which we spend energy, and the manner of our speech. Also, attention should be focused on the way we breathe, our hygiene habits and addictive habits if they are part of our personal reality.

The physical body should be maintained in a clean condition, well hydrated and fed with a healthy, balanced diet in moderation, since anything in excess ends up being harmful. Meal times should be considered sacred rituals conducted, if possible, in silence, peace, harmony, in full consciousness of the vital energy (prana) the aliments provide, and a sentiment of gratitude for the food itself and for all the beings that one way or another participated in the production of our meal. Sufficient time should be allotted in order to chew well and extensively. It is best to keep beverages (water) for a while in the mouth before swallowing. All this ensures that greater amounts of vital energy (prana), and not only chemicals, will be liberated from the substances we ingest.

To remain verbally silent during meal times is not enough. Any kind of adverse, bitter thoughts and sentiments during a meal should best be eliminated. Grateful and loving thoughts have the power of penetrating the matter of the aliments, freeing all cosmic subtle energies contained therein and allowing our body to absorb them.

Also, it would be beneficial for our health if we could observe periods of fasting. In addition to the spiritual benefits of fasting, such as facilitating meditation and contemplative states as well as bringing us closer to God and the spiritual world, it induces purification of the physical body through the slowing down of certain cellular functions. Thus giving the cells the chance to rest and be peaceful, entering the "great silence" which later is transferred to our whole being.

In the same fashion, we must learn to become fully conscious of the implications involved in the simple, involuntary act of breathing. It is ceaseless life brought to us in the form not only of oxygen, but of vital energy (prana). Therefore, engaging in the conscious practice of deep breathing exercises does tremendously invigorate the physical body. It is necessary to bring the inhaled air all the way down to the base of the lungs in order to obtain maximum amounts of prana to be absorbed by our body.

On one hand, the physical body must have sufficient action, provided by the practice of different physical exercises, which would maintain a healthy state of bones, joints and muscles. This also promotes the proper functioning of the human circulatory systems such as the arterial, venous, lymphatic and pranic or energetic. On the other hand, the physical body also needs appropriate rest from all activities, physical and mental, and sleeping periods that would allow for recovering, regeneration of tissues, and the emotional/mental balancing mechanism provided by dreaming activity. A perfect balance and equilibrium must be found between activity and rest.

Sexual manifestation should be undertaken as well, as a sacred ritual dedicated to the creator and performed with the ingredients of care, love and trust. It is the nature of thoughts, attitude and the quality of energy exchanged between the partners that make the sexual act a sacred one. It is in the heart and in the thoughts that the expression of physical love can transcend all limitations. If we can look at each other as representations of the divine principles that created the world, the Father and Mother aspects of God, we could transcend the ordinary limitations of sexual relationships and transform them into luminous and pure experiences, full of respect and veneration. Thus, the union is consummated at a higher level, when both partners are literally channels conducting and exchanging divine energy.Furthermore, each and every of our usual activities must be considered sacred and we should encourage ourselves to remain with full consciousness in the present moment while performing them.

Of outmost importance is to observe and correct the way in which we express ourselves by means of the spoken word, since words carry very powerful energy that could either harm or encourage others. We must learn to know when it is the appropriate moment to speak and how to do it. We must learn to speak in a positive way; to help and encourage, not hurting or belittling others. We must eliminate false promises or commitments, false flattery, gossip, harmful criticism, manipulation, and control or exerting influence for our benefit with our words. We must learn to really listen, with all our being, to our words as well as other's.

In the end all addictions must be eliminated, since they take away our power and will converting us into puppets and damaging our physical health. And, when I refer to addictions, I do not mean only alcohol, tobacco and drugs, but also medications, food, promiscuous sex, telephones, television and computers.

To aid the purification process of the physical body as well as the purification of the other principles (emotional and mental), it is very important to work consciously and purposely on the etheric body or energy body so that both blocks and leaks of energy, that induce disharmony, can be corrected and thus abundant currents of prana are allowed to flow freely throughout the different bodies of our constitution, securing a good state of health at all levels.

Going through the innumerable experiences of our material lives we must interact with other beings and the surrounding environment. Our actions, reactions and mental attitude in this game of contact and exchange, inevitably at some point, create both blocks as well as spills of prana or vital energy from the etheric body, which affects negatively the free circulation of energy through this system. From the former statement we can infer that we are totally responsible for each and all the consequences that manifest in our being.

The focal central points of vital energy along the spinal cord of a human being, known by the name of "chakras," have energetic domain over all levels (physical – emotional – mental – spiritual) at their corresponding area of activity. In any situation in which the normal energy flow of this system is altered, the result is either or both, a congestion or a decrease of vital energy in certain areas of the human structure at all the levels encompassed by the specific energy center or chakra. The outcome in these cases is invariably disharmony that manifests, sooner or later, as disease. This is the consequence of excluding that area from the healthy functioning of the whole.

So we conclude that the presence of clogging or leaking within the energy system deleteriously affects the totality of levels of our being and retards our spiritual growth. For this very important reason, it is fundamental we get to work in order to dissipate the obstructions and seal the leaks within our energy system, and reestablish a healthy flow of vital energy through our different bodies of manifestation.

For us to be capable of doing this kind of work with ourselves, we need to acquire knowledge about these energy centers and their functions. This will assist us in the process of discovering problems at different levels of our constitution and give us an orientation as to how to proceed in the direction of solving them and achieve healing. Our goal is to render the different lower bodies operating in harmony with each other and connected to the higher bodies; in this manner the lower bodies will be constantly invigorated by a ceaseless stream of vital energy, which in turn will result in further awakening of consciousness since the chakras are depositaries of varied levels of consciousness within the individual.

The following are questions we must pose to ourselves in order to discover and know if we have problems at the level of the first or Root Chakra (representing "group power" and "survival instinct") that we need to solve and take care of:

- Do we experience a decrease in physical energy, or anemia, or bowels and rectal difficulties or bones and muscles problems? (Physical/material level).
- Do we find difficulties in surviving? Such as, for instance, not finding or losing jobs? (Physical/material level).
- Do we feel disconnected from nature? (Physical/material level)
- Do we feel isolated from others and society? (Physical/material level)
- Do we suffer from depression and fears? For instance, fear of losing possessions and money? (Emotional level).
- Do we find ourselves being insecure, unstable and lacking self confidence? (Mental level).
- Do we have lack of courage and will power? (Mental level).
- Do we exhibit difficulty with persevering and enduring? (Mental level).
- Do we have the habit of blaming circumstances or others? (Mental level).
- Do we often experience problematic relationships with family members? (Emotional/mental level).
- Do we think that our own race, culture, religion, country, or political orientation is the best as opposed to others? (Mental level).
- Do we exhibit prejudice in our behavior? (Mental level).

In working to find out problems at the level of the second or Sacral Chakra (representing "relationship power," deep emotions and creativity) we ought to ask the following questions:

- Do we have sexual problems, or suffer illnesses of the sexual organs, kidneys and bladder? (Physical level).
- Do we feel anxious, frustrated, or experience feelings of jealousy or vengeance? (Emotional/mental level).
- Are we markedly attached to others? (Emotional/mental level).
- Is it hard for us to be aware and relate to our own feelings? (Emotional/mental level).
- Are we poor in creativity and taking the lead? (Mental level).
- Are we excessively impatient? (Mental level).
- Do we have a problem promoting and accepting our own well-being? (Emotional/mental level).

- Do we manifest imbalance in our one-to-one relationship with others? For instance, wanting to dominate another or the opposite, letting ourselves be controlled by another.

In regard to the   (representing "individual power" and outer expression of emotions) the questions would be:

- Do we have to deal with disturbances of the stomach, pancreas, liver or gall bladder? (Physical/material level).
- Do we often feel angry? (Emotional level).
- Are we the victims of greed, doubt or guilt? (Emotional/mental level).
- Do we feel lacking power as individuals? (Emotional/mental level).
- Do we lack in ambition and self confidence? (Mental level).
- Do we have problems in our profession and work area?(Emotional/mental level).
- Do we have difficulties in taking responsibility and making commitments? (Mental level).
- Do we manipulate others for our own gains? (Mental level).
- Are we incapable of sustaining our promises? (Mental level).
- Do we depend too much on the opinion of others? (Mental level).
- Do we really respect ourselves? (Mental level).

The fourth or Heart Chakra represents our "love power" and the questions to be formulated at this level are:

- Do we experience illnesses of the heart, blood pressure, circulatory system, or lungs? (Physical/material level).
- Do we lack in sensitivity and compassion? (Emotional level).
- Do we show a tendency to be sorrowful and gloomy? (Emotional level).
- Are we emotionally aloof? (Emotional level).
- Do we experience resentment and lack in forgiving? (Emotional/mental level).
- Do we have problems letting go of negative experiences of the past? (Emotional/mental level).
- Do we really love ourselves enough? (Emotional level).
- Do we verily know how to give and receive love? (Emotional level).
- Do we truly accept others as they are? (Mental level).

Questions related to the fifth or Throat Chakra (representing "will power" and expression of creativity) are:

- Do we face problems with our throat, voice, or thyroid gland? (Physical/material level).
- Are we prone to feel grief or shame? (Emotional/mental level).Do we experience difficulty in expressing our needs and wants, or our creative impulses? (Emotional/mental level).
- Do we have problem communicating?(Emotional/mental level).
- Are we really honest and truthful? (Mental level).
- Do we lack self-control? (Mental level).
- Are we victims of obsessions or addictions? (Emotional/mental level).
- Are we capable of making proper decisions in our lives that will encourage spiritual growth? (Mental level).
- Are we positively supporting and stimulating others? (Mental level).
- Do we verily know to accept whatever is and align our will to that of God's? (Emotional/mental level).

The sixth or Third Eye Chakra represents the "power of mind" and spiritual vision. In order to discover any block at this level we must ask ourselves the following:

- Do we have ailments of the eyes, ears, or nose? (Physical/material level).
- Do we feel disconnected from people? (Emotional/mental level).
- Do we feel confused or cannot think properly? (Mental level).
- Are we using only our intellectual capacity, disconnected from feelings and heart? ; or, are we not sufficiently stimulated intellectually? (Mental level).
- Are we narrow minded and judgmental? (Mental level).
- Are we open sufficiently to new ideas and different opportunities? (Mental level).
- Do we lack in imagination? (Mental level).
- Do we pay attention to our intuitive capacity? (Mental level).
- Do we inquire enough and seek spiritual truths? (Mental level).

In relation to the seventh or Crown Chakra level (representing the "power of spirit" and cosmic link) we may ask the following:

- Do we have nervous system problems, headaches or mental problems? (Physical/mental level).
- Are we depressed, or constantly preoccupied, or obsessed about something? (Emotional/mental level).
- Are we closing ourselves to spirituality and cosmic connections? (Emotional/mental level).
- Do we practice meditation and prayer? (Emotional/mental level).
- Are we capable of having and maintaining faith? (Emotional/mental level).
- Are we authentically humble and grateful? (Emotional/mental level).
- Do we realize our purpose in life on Earth? (Mental level).

In the average person these energy centers are minimally active and between them we find dense nets of etheric substance which function as consciousness obstructions. Due to progressive spiritual development and growth, which results in energy rising from the lower chakras, these compact areas between the chakras little by little disintegrate, thus permitting the individual to access higher levels of consciousness and finally the possibility of operating in a state of "unbroken consciousness," that is continuous total awareness at all levels of being.

So, through deliberate spiritual work the chakras enlarge, their rotation speed increases considerably, their colors turn more brilliant and translucent, and their connected energy channels open one by one. Consequently, the electromagnetic field (aura) of the person expands greatly, exhibiting harmonious and beautiful geometrical conformations that vibrate in consonance with the totality of creation.

Thus, to serve our purpose, we must consciously work in order to open, unclog, invigorate and fully expand all the central energy centers or chakras, especially at the levels where we discover problems. We can do this by means of direct application of colors, fragrances, stones/crystals, sound vibrations (tuning forks), or microcrystal plates on the corresponding chakra areas. In addition, we can do this by practicing meditation, creative imagination, energy exercises, breathing exercises, mantra chanting, dream work, and listening to crystal or metal bell vibrations. Also we have the choice of asking for help in this task by consulting a knowledgeable person in the use of the pendulum and in working on the human electromagnetic field of energy.

For a more detailed explanation of how to work for the development of the chakras, the reader is referred to the first volume of Compendium of Metaphysics: "The Human Being – Physical and Etheric Bodies."

Above all we should work extensively to transform for the better our mental attitude, emotional reactions and physical actions.

In a general manner, when the vital energy contained in both the first or Root Chakra and the second or Sacral Chakra is balanced and commanded wisely by the energy contained in the   , the process of chakra energy rising commences, as illustrated in Diagram #5. The level of consciousness gradually shifts from ego-selfishness to the expression of all-inclusive love. This consciousness of expanded love begins to direct the mind and will of the person. The whole process of magnification of consciousness can bring the individual from the condition of birth and survival struggle while incarnated to the state of full liberation.

In reality, the complete process represents what is known as "the rising of Kundalini energy," which is stored, in a dormant state, within the first or Root Chakra and must be awakened during the course of spiritual advancement. Kundalini is manifested as the confluence of three different forces:

- "Fohat" that represents the Father aspect of the Holy Trinity or the Monadic Spiritual Will carried by the First Cosmic Ray of creation.
- "Prana," the vital energy of life that represents the Son/Daughter aspect of the Holy Trinity or Consciousness/Wisdom carried by the Second Cosmic Ray of creation.
- "Shakti" that represents the Mother aspect of the Holy Trinity or the Intelligence/Power inherent in matter (atomic energy) carried by the Third Cosmic Ray of creation.

Kundalini embodies, in the human being, the equivalent to the divine powers of creation/destruction/regeneration. Eventually, when the human being is ready, through conscious spiritual work and successive magnifications of consciousness, these three energies constituting the tremendous force we call Kundalini, shall rise in unison under the influence and stimulus of the Monadic Spiritual Will of the individual (the highest manifestation of the will or Father aspect) thus fully and completely awakening each chakra on its ascending path through the main central energy channels. When they reach the seventh or Crown Chakra they merge into their cosmic counterparts and the outcome of this is what we call "enlightenment" of the individual.

Along the line of self-correction and transformation it is very likely that many times we may fall back into old habits that we were trying to eliminate. This should not be taken as a failure on our part and we should persist in trying again and again, as long as necessary. Any apparent defeat, in reality, is not so for the simple reason that there is always a lesson to learn behind it and some good to be gained from it. Only perseverance, patience and encouragement are necessary. The real power to make us healthier is within each one of us and every time we try again to correct something in ourselves, we have a new chance to make it right. We must become totally conscious of this truth!

With time, the work we do on ourselves will succeed in expelling out completely all coarser materials and thus rendering the physical body into a lighter and more refined structure, with a faster vibratory frequency and possessing a nervous system capable of responding readily to the higher vibrations approaching from the spiritual bodies via the soul extension.

In summary: In order to be successful in accomplishing the modification of our physical negative habits it is necessary first of all to become clearly aware of them; then, instruction, understanding, firm determination and the use of personal will power.

The next steps bring us to initiate work at emotional/mental levels, since our thoughts have the power of either vivify or destroy us. This work entails changing or erasing old emotional/mental patterns of energy that are rigidly recorded in the subconscious part of the mind and are no longer useful for our spiritual advancement. Even more, they are harmful and threatening to our physical, emotional and mental balance and good health.

Certainly we leak and lose vital energy through engaging in excessive sexual activity, addictions, compulsive/obsessive behavior or abusive behavior, gossiping, criticizing, thinking of revenge, thinking as a victim or the contrary, victimizing others; as well as having feelings of envy, jealousy, greed, fear and guilt. In these ways we are misdirecting the vital energy flow through our being and depleting ourselves of the energy that could have been utilized in a favorable and more creative manner. That is why it becomes necessary, a priority, to transform ourselves toward a positive end by modifying what we need rather than pointing at other's apparent defects.

We ought to re-think and re-evaluate our entire value system and tray to eliminate the old patterns that maintain the brain circuits of undesirable learned behaviors. While we are still spiritually undeveloped we follow mechanically our automatic emotional/physical reactions which manifest repeatedly, following roads of least resistance. In this primitive condition our thoughts are mainly shaped by those basic emotions. Nonetheless, in facing any given life situation, we always have the opportunity to make a more conscious choice, beyond any automatic reaction. We possess the capacity to overcome primitive states, change old patterns of automatic responses, and use properly the power of thought over the physical/emotional aspects. Otherwise, by reacting impulsively, we are not in the right position to resolve any disturbing or chaotic situation in our lives. The manner in which we respond to persons and circumstances of life is a direct indicator of our level of wisdom and sense of humor.

I will illustrate the former with an example: If we come to face a situation or the actions of another person that provokes us to feel anger, even if this feeling could be justified, we have two options of behavior available, or maybe three: 1 – We allow ourselves to be dominated by the feeling of anger and express it with some kind of violence, either verbal or even physical, with the consequence of producing harm to others and self. 2 – We repress completely or partially the feeling of anger, bringing deleterious effects to self. 3 – We intelligently decide to look at things in a really profound manner (the situation, the person, ourselves). Then it is possible to see more clearly and perhaps resolve to be forgiving or not act under the effect of the strong emotion of anger and rather discuss things over. The latest scenario certainly will result in more benign consequences.

Our emotions are important from several points of view:

- They show us where we stand on the road of evolution and point us the way to correction.
- They offer us the opportunity to exert our free will of choice.
- They allow us to experience the magical side of living here, in this manifestation of reality.

When we talk about working with our emotions, we are referring not to deny them but, on the contrary, to feel them, acknowledge them and learn the proper way to deal with them. This way will be: feel, see, breathe deeply, and then release their energy, allowing it to flow without any judgment. The continuous, moving flow of energy throughout our being is a very important determinant of our state of general health at all levels. We must learn to use our life force in a beneficial manner conducive toward spiritual development and creativity.

Of fundamental value is the practice of true forgiveness toward others, as much as toward ourselves. If we retain within ourselves grudge and rancor, we will be detaining the easy flow of vital energy and thus creating blocks. Therefore, for our own benefit, resentment and negative feelings should be let go.

Again, on the face of any "negative emotion," we are presented with the choices of:

- Denying our feelings or ignoring them completely, with the consequent outcome of stagnant and harmful energy accumulated within our system.
- Reacting automatically and committing harmful acts toward others and consequently also toward ourselves.
- Feeling it, acknowledging it without opinions or condemnation, and finally releasing it.

On the face of "positive emotions," we should act on those feelings that reinforce spiritual growth.

Why is it so important for us to accomplish a state of mind that will allow us to make right choices? Simply because the nature of our choices determines the conditions of our lives, our state of health and have effects on others as well, including the entire creation. Isn't it a tremendous responsibility? Well, we must now assume it.

Thus, we must work in order to banish or transform emotional and mental negative habits, which are undesirable if we expect further spiritual growth. From the emotional point of view we want to work with the so called "negative emotions" and reactions; and from the mental point of view, we must work with the so called "negative thoughts," false beliefs, distorted perceptions and lack of knowledge. If we are ignorant about certain spiritual truths, we will entertain false beliefs and thoughts which contribute to twist and deform our perception of the surrounding reality (seen as well as unseen) and consequently, the end result will be making wrong decisions.

Again, this task can be accomplished by using awareness, courage, knowledge, comprehension, perseverance, will power and proper activity of the lower mind which manifests when we are capable of connecting with our soul extension and allowing it to direct the mind through what we call "intuitive capacity." In this manner, the lower mind becomes brightened and clear to aid in the process of transmutation and real growth of the individual. Basically and ideally, the intellect should serve only for pointing us to the best way (right choice), and always guided by the heart (soul/spirit). The intellect is a very useful tool for us to prepare optimal conditions and to carry us through the beginning of the spiritual path. However, there is a limit beyond which the intellect cannot take us further.

The intellect helps us to be vigilant and to find out the negative patterns we manifest. It helps us to make the decision to eliminate them and reinforce those attitudes that are beneficial. But when the intellect reaches its limit, should humbly yield to the guidance of the intuitive capacity. That is why we must connect with and develop this capacity through becoming very responsive to the soul. Intuition is a higher form of intelligence which brings us direct and total knowledge of the truth at each step we take. Complete knowledge is born from the fusion of intelligence and sensitivity. Intuition is nothing more than a form of divine guidance that manifests when we have learned to verily "listen" and "feel." When we fully honor our intuitive capacity, then we may lead a life in harmony with the entire cosmos and God.

Above all, we must be totally willing to change and free ourselves from past blocks that impede our path and delay our growth, by letting go and releasing all harmful habitual behaviors. Mainly we must learn to let go of unhealthy emotional patterns that cloud our mind. The manner in which we can do this work is by taking one by one, and one at a time each, all the negative habits we have discovered in the functioning of our personality through the previous self-observation and analysis, with the goal in mind to eliminate or transmute them into their opposite quality, as well as change the contents of our old "mental recordings."

We must try to track back each negative component of our personality to the starting point, so we are able to understand its source of origin and reasons, since this is extremely important to allow us to solve our present problems. This work is done by reviewing our life from the times our memory permits, as well as by asking for help in the manner of hypnosis or past life regression therapy. In this process, the practice of meditation trains us to become receptive to the guidance from our soul/spirit. Also we have available directions from our dreams and, through prayer we may request higher divine leading as well.

Further work on self-correction must be done on the following areas:

— We must <u>stop criticizing, judging and condemning</u> others, including ourselves, since this is a way of separating people, of classifying things into "bad" and "good," "superior" and "inferior." We must try hard to keep in mind the fact that we are all at different stages on the evolutionary process. Everybody is doing the best they can do given their degree of development and understanding. We must remind ourselves that what the personality does,(the three lower bodies playing the game of planetary life), never can change or alter what the human being in reality is: a divine spark of spirit. We must learn to look beyond the personality and appearance, straight to that spark that is inevitably present within each one of us. We must learn to be totally respectful to others, without any distinctions and learn to eliminate gossip from our vocabulary as well.

— We must <u>learn to be flexible while keeping balance and harmony in giving and receiving</u>, in all exchanges with all the kingdoms of nature. Since life is ever continuous change and movement, by being flexible we can better accommodate to these inescapable changes. It is a good practice to be willing to try and know new things, different to the ones we grew accustomed to. This brakes rigidity and helps us to advance beyond our limitations. In order to maintain a balanced state of being, it is important for us to learn which activities of ours drain our energy uselessly, and which ones, on the contrary, recharge us with vital force due to their positive and benign nature. Furthermore, we must learn to keep a balance between the surrounding external world and our internal world. We must never get totally immersed in external activities and cut the connection with the inner world, since this is the center that provides all true nourishment, vitality and strength. This really constitutes the source of all life.

— We must <u>learn to truly listen</u>. Listen to ourselves internally as well as externally, listen to others, listen to nature and listen to the Divine. In order to really listen, the primordial condition is silence. We must learn to reach a state of deep silence to be able to listen to anything. To attain this state we ought to elevate ourselves internally, to subtler and higher regions where our vision becomes clearer, creativity flows in freedom, and true understanding and knowing meet us. Knowing how to be in silence allows us to review our lives and learn from it. Inevitably it faces us with our inner disorders and from there we can better decide the necessary changes to be done. Another positive effect of silence is that our energy will be recharged and renovated. The state of silence requires a state of harmony at the three lower levels: physical, emotional and lower mental. Once the supreme state of silence is attained, we are guided by spirit and we can listen to the voice of the Divine.

— We must <u>learn to admit our mistakes and errors</u> and be willing to try again, with the help of spirit.

— We must <u>learn to release or let go at all levels</u>; that is, learn to be prepared for the unavoidable changes in life. This implies to release the past, completely immerse oneself in the now, welcome the unknown and abandon all attachments. Also we must learn to let go totally both, the need for control or approval from others. In addition, we should let go old and rigid beliefs that would prevent us from advancing and expanding.

- We should <u>practice remaining completely conscious of all the details of our daily activities (including our manner of speech, actions and moments of silence), our attitude and thoughts, as well as our emotional reactions</u> related to others and our own circumstances. We must come out of automatic, mechanical functioning. We ought to observe our thoughts and attitudes of: non trust, manipulation, intimidation, or control toward others; and these must be corrected. Remaining aware will help us to uncover fears, blocks and leaks of energy, weaknesses and strengths we possess.

- We must <u>try to practice being fully aware of every event and external circumstance</u> surrounding us. This modality aids in the process of realizing our direction and purpose in living, as well as identifying karmic situations we need to balance in the present life.

- We must <u>learn to see the link between our actions/reactions/attitudes and their consequences</u>. If we are successful in doing this, we will be learning more about one of the most important universal laws: the Karmic Law. We must become absolutely cognizant that the totality of events in our life is a straight consequence or result of our thoughts, feelings and actions. In this manner, we learn to make proper choices to steer our life in the right direction, correcting the imbalances and chaos we generate.

- We must <u>learn complete surrender and acceptance of what it is right now</u>, since this is part of a superior Will that knows better than our little will. We must stop lamenting and rebelling against the present situation. Instead we should accept and then take action if any is required for the better. We must find the way to get accustomed to see the favorable and positive of each circumstance in our lives and in each person we encounter. Everything that happens to us represents a lesson to learn. We are all students/teachers and therefore we must be thankful toward everything and person life faces us to. Neither situation nor person can be negative in its totality. There would be always something good that can be rescued, even if invisible to our ordinary eyes. Hence the need to learn to look for the positive, for this practice can drive our thoughts and feelings away from the negative.If we do this, we will be constantly aligned with cosmic energy flow which will re-vitalize us. So we should try to look for the hidden benefits in every problem or difficulty we must face in life.

- We should <u>be reverent of the sacred</u>, which is all life. We should maintain an absolutely conscious contact and exchange with the sacred elements of nature and its kingdoms. Carefully observing the ways in which nature functions brings us one of the best teaching tools. We must keep firmly a learning attitude toward nature.

- Of outmost importance is to <u>acknowledge the Creator, or that energy we call God</u>. We should recognize and feel that our life has a purpose and is inevitably linked to and fed by a higher power or divine energy through our soul/spirit; even if this is not yet understood with the mind.

- We must be <u>eternally grateful</u> for everything we have (including our very life), and for everything that happens in our life; even the hard circumstances since these are challenges offering us new opportunities to advance our learning, our awakening, and to increase our inner strength.

- We must try to <u>bring about, into our present, loving feelings, laughter and joy</u>. We must attempt to learn joyfully than otherwise, for this helps us to liberate stacked energy and brings forward lightness which promotes healing. It is important to learn to laugh at ourselves and be humorous about certain things such as our own self-importance, pride, sense of uniqueness and preoccupations.

- We must <u>learn to live in total harmony and synchrony with the entirety of cosmic life</u>.

- We must <u>become sensitive enough to recognize and correctly interpret the messages that life brings us from the invisible world and respond accordingly to them</u>. The purpose of these messages is to wake us up in case we are being negligent with our spiritual work of transformation and growth. They will come to us if we ignore or are lazy to learn our lessons and they may take, sometimes, drastic forms such as near-death experiences, an illness, or severe losses; something to really shake us up. Also, these messages may come in the form of gentle guidance for us, when we seem to be deviating from our spiritual path. If we do not pay heed to these messages, challenges in our life will increase in number and magnitude until the time when we do learn.
- We ought to <u>correct erroneous perception of reality</u>, especially about our real Selves that are primordial sparks of spirit and light, not only dense physical bodies.
- Another fundamental aim of our work should be to <u>accomplish the proper use of our divine attributes of will, love, thoughts, choice and action</u>, which will then demonstrate as:

  - Will to do always good.
  - Thoughts being positive and creative in nature.
  - Choices conducive to spiritual advancement.
  - Love that is inclusive of everything and expresses as compassion.
  - Actions guided by wisdom and expressed as cooperation instead of competition. These can be considered as positive actions.

The persistent work to change our negative habits making use of our will power consciously at first, later on becomes an effortless, spontaneous exhibition of our capacity to make proper decisions on the spiritual course of advancement. This may be a slow process, to be done stage by stage. That is why we must call to the fore all the patience we are capable of.

Why do we want to correct ourselves at all levels? Simply because it is our true duty to reach the goal of using our lower bodies (physical – emotional – lower mental) solely in function of the soul extension which is the messenger from our spiritual bodies and only serves a higher purpose for us. Therefore, our necessary and immediate task should be to concern ourselves with the transformation of our lower vehicles of manifestation in a manner that they become purified and completely responsive to the promptings of the soul/spirit. The forms/ vehicles/ bodies which carry consciousness must be progressively evolved in order to be absolutely capable of supporting higher states of consciousness.

We must work on ourselves in order to unify our lower bodies and align them with soul/spirit, so that all of them function and move following only one direction: the Divine World, the unique point toward which all our faculties and activities must converge. The only goal for our physical, emotional, mental bodies and soul should be illumination and perfection. Any manifestation of spirit is going to be limited by the condition of the lower vehicles (physical – emotional – lower mental). Therefore the matter or form must never be neglected and our first concern on the spiritual path must be how to purify and transform our lower bodies in a manner that they would absorb, become, and radiate light. Only then the spiritual virtues could be exhibited through these bodies. So we work on matter to transmute and spiritualize it.

We ourselves have created the obstacles we must surmount. With our inferior thoughts, attitudes, feelings and actions we have built dense layers around us, which obstruct all channels and cut all communication with higher levels of existence. We have isolated and separated ourselves. Although in reality we are submerged in pure light, this cannot penetrate to us and we cannot feel it. Only purification and sensitization of our lower bodies can restore their receptivity and the seemingly interrupted communication with more elevated spiritual levels. This allows the free circulation of divine light through us and the profound realization that indeed there is no separation between matter and spirit, or the realization of that spark of spirit existing within each human being and in each aspect of creation. We must toil tirelessly to harmoniously evolve the triangle of our physical body, heart (emotions), and intellect (mind). In this way we achieve the purity of a limpid crystal that automatically allows the penetration and passage of divine light.

During this process of self-transformation or of remodeling ourselves, we are more than likely bound to experience certain uncomfortable symptoms at all levels of our being that cannot be explained from a traditional medical point of view. All these different sensations are due to energy changes resulting from this ongoing metamorphosis. An energetic re-wiring process is happening within our nervous system, producing the activation of formerly unused neurological paths through new connections established between neuron cells in the brain. This is happening in order to prepare the individual to receive new levels of awareness and expansion of the present degree of consciousness.

These symptoms may vary from person to person and they may comprise the following:

- Unusual headaches and insomnia
- Shaking or feeling of bouncing
- Muscle cramps
- Shooting pains in the limbs
- Shortness of breath for no reason
- Pressure in the chest
- Weakness or on the other hand, outbursts of energy
- Tingling sensation in different parts of the body
- Dizziness
- Nauseas
- Sudden outbreak of points of light in front of the eyes
- Light drops falling on us or in front of us
- The surfacing of certain fears that have been engraved in the cellular memory of the body
- Eruptions of inspiration
- Sense of disorientation with an altered perception of space/time
- Losing the desire to be in groups and crowds
- Lose of sexual desire
- Increased sensitivity to the point of not tolerating any kind of loud argument or violence in any form, even reading or watching it in movies

What is happening in reality is that two worlds are becoming in closer contact, the external physical world and the internal spiritual world. We are learning and adapting to live consciously in both, in unison. Our physical bodies are becoming accustomed to circulate higher cosmic energy through them. This is the process during which our physical, emotional and mental bodies are closely reconnected with our primordial spiritual essence: our Monad. This would allow us to experience different levels of cosmic awareness, or expansions of consciousness, and thus we become clear conduits for neutral universal energy that we must ground on Earth.

When we are going through this process of transformation and experience any of the previously mentioned symptoms, we must try to conserve energy, slow down, not panic, remain at the center of our being calmly, and not push the physical body beyond its endurance capacity, which would be reduced at this point. If we do not respect this, illness may develop.

The final result of this arduous alchemical labor will be the complete purification and harmonious blending of the lower bodies that constitute our personality. When we finally transform ourselves in this way, our overall energy rises to pure levels of consciousness and we emanate light/wisdom that influences and inspires others to follow these steps toward spiritual growth. Wisdom manifests when a pure mind and heart are blended and used in equal measures. And yes, our interior state of being does not concern only us but also affect others. The only veritable manner of helping humanity is by becoming a center of purity ourselves and irradiate light outward, which will contribute for the betterment of everybody around.

When we reach this condition of purity, we are able to recapture the wonder and innocence of children. On the contrary, if we remain in an impure state that is fostering negativity, greed, selfishness and injustice, we will be contributing to poisoning our world.

6 Developing the Practice of Spiritual Disciplines

- Prayers can attract the attention of higher cosmic consciousnesses that will provide help, teaching, and guidance for us.
- The practice of moments of silence helps the mind to learn stillness. It purifies the mind.
- The practice of creative imagination can be used to re-create circumstances and ourselves with the power of imagination and thus expanding consciousness.
- The practice of meditation opens us to receive guidance and healing, producing a magnification of our consciousness when we become directly or experientially cognizant of the presence of soul/spirit within us.
- The practice of chanting mantras allows us to invoke certain states of consciousness and offer us purifying vibrations.
- The practice of dream work helps in the process of discovering weaknesses, fears, blocks and leaks of vital energy, as well as good and strong qualities in ourselves. It also brings about healing and provides guidance for the work we must do with ourselves.
- The practice of Yoga and energy exercises reinforces the power of concentration and focusing. Also, it activates all the energy centers or chakras and helps to develop the quality of patience. It is a powerful aid for the proper alignment of the lower bodies to the higher ones.
- The practice of encountering others mainly at the level of spirit and not solely at personality level (lower bodies) implicates learning to see others as the spirit spark that we all are. We must honor spirit in everyone and in every part of nature's kingdoms.

7 Engaging in the practice of assistance to others (service) without being bound by the expectancy of recognition, approval or reward. This would be the ultimate expression of love for humanity in a broad sense, without admitting any kind of separation. At some point on the road, we will start to feel the desire to serve. Then, we should commit to be of service to humanity by offering and sharing our talents and moving beyond selfish, limiting interests and ideals. By helping others we learn to look at our own problems differently and our self-perception of being victims may shift considerably.

So, recapitulating, all the work we must do to improve ourselves and grow spiritually is aimed to the purification of the lower bodies (physical – emotional – lower mental), and the construction of a moral character. Propitiously, this would assist in modifying our basic temperament and little by little allow the concrete expression of divinity, carried on by the soul extension through purified vehicles.

The tools we first employ for this task are: intelligence, will power and the force of our strengths; the goal being to transform our weaknesses into positive qualities, vanish all fear, and finally reach a point where the entirety of our actions are guided by wisdom which is the final product from the right union of mind and heart or knowledge and love. In this manner, all workings of the mind allow the heart to intervene, in unison and in balance. Our alchemical transformation leads to the concrete expression of the totality of our spiritual potential as human beings, through the different stages of consciousness magnification. We can consciously accelerate this happening when we discover that this is our only purpose in living: to acknowledge and use our strong qualities, to work on the transformation of our weaknesses and balance of our karmic debts, to learn different lessons, to find harmony and balance, to extend love and progress through expansions of consciousness (awakening) toward our pristine and original state of oneness.

SYNTHESIS

- Our temperament (basic instincts and tendencies) could change positively through our conscious work aiming to improve and build our character along innumerable planetary life periods or reincarnations.
- The development of character entails:
  - Acquiring knowledge of our true constitution and relation to the whole (entire cosmos).
  - Self-observation and analysis of ourselves at all levels.
  - Accurate and honest conclusion about ourselves (awareness of our weak and strong points).
  - Strong and steady determination to work on ourselves.
  - Doing the actual work of self-correction by purifying the physical, emotional and mental bodies; that is eliminating deleterious physical, emotional and mental habits. Also, eliminating blocks and leaks from the energy system, developing and awakening the chakras or energy centers, stopping all judgments, releasing and letting go old unnecessary patterns, surrendering to spirit, encouraging joy, gratefulness and reverence, trying to harmonize with cosmic forces, developing total mindfulness in daily activities and becoming absolutely aware of the link between our actions and its consequences.
  - Practicing spiritual disciplines (prayer – meditation – moments of silence – creative imagination – mantra chanting – dream work).
  - Practicing energy exercises or Yoga.
  - Learning to encounter others at the level of spirit only.
  - Practicing service to humanity.
- The aim of this work should be to attain transformation for the better by modifying our mental attitude, emotional reactions and physical actions. Our duty is to render our lower bodies working only in function of the soul extension that serves the higher purpose of spirit.
- Our sole purpose in living is:
  - Discover weak and strong points in the makeup of our being.
  - Work conscientiously to eliminate and transform our weaknesses.
  - Balance karmic forces.
  - Learn lessons and find harmony.
  - Progress, through expansions of consciousness, beyond duality toward our original state of oneness.

CHAPTER VI

INITIATIONS

Along the process of conscious spiritual work, we awaken our consciousness to progressively expanded levels. Each time we reach a crucial point where we have completed a certain round of experiences and related learning; by having absorbed that learning, having passed different pertinent tests, and becoming capable of practically demonstrating all our knowledge as well as prepared and ready for further advancement and greater spiritual growth, we take an "initiation."

Initiations mark increasing degrees of purification, unification and integration of light within our being. Externally, we take our initiations on the inner planes of existence while inhabiting our "dream bodies" (astral bodies). We attend a ritual conducted by the higher spiritual beings of our planetary hierarchy, where we are exposed to high currents of energy that would augment the overall vibratory frequency of our being, energize our soul extension, and rearrange our atomic structure. Also, during initiations, we receive certain truths or revelations that will help us to further our spiritual progress. Thus we now stand ready to face a new cycle of experiences, studies, discoveries, tests and practices. We may or may not be able to bring to physical consciousness the occurrence of these rituals; and most of the times we are not aware of them taking place at all.

Through the process of initiations, we can progressively discover all the mysteries surrounding the whole of creation (cosmos) and the grand importance of our role and participation within it. Thus we escalate to higher degrees of awareness or awakening of our consciousness. Along this way we are steered in the direction of awakening "group consciousness" which involves cooperation and sharing. We realize we must flow with and support the Divine Plan, and advance to the completion of our planetary task of demonstrating the harmonious and unified functioning of the three divine aspects we carry within: Will/Power/Purpose, Love/Wisdom and Active Intelligence of God. With this accomplishment, we walk through life while sustaining a conscious and full link with all the levels of the spiritual world. This process represents the road of ascension from the fourth kingdom of nature (Human kingdom) to the fifth Spiritual kingdom at the planetary hierarchy level.

So our spiritual evolution takes place by undergoing several initiations over the span of many life periods or reincarnations. The challenges we confront through this awakening and transformative process takes us through the initiations. Since we are going to be tested on our weaknesses, we must learn how to use our strengths and discover what we ought to let go from our lives in order to triumph over our limitations. Thus in the physical world, life itself is a continuous thread of initiations (minor and major). We have to learn to find equilibrium between the outer experiences and the internal ways of our soul, amalgamating the spiritual world with the daily life of our existence. We grow and advance through the opportunities of choice life presents us with. We wound ourselves and lose vital energy when we choose wrongly. However, if we fail to respond (choose) correctly (to aid spiritual growth), we always can choose again and again and again….. There are infinite chances to correct, along many lifetimes. Also, in order to progress as human beings, we need to pull to the fore an unwavering willingness to awaken and become our full potential for divinity.

Within our solar system there are nine initiations to be taken on the spiritual path of awakening consciousness, seven of which can be taken on the plane of our planet Earth, and are called "planetary initiations." Here, in our school Earth, we evolve through the seven sub planes of the Physical Cosmic Plane of existence. These sub planes are linked to the seven levels of initiation we must pass through:

- The <u>first initiation</u> is attained when we acquire expertise over the Physical or Objective sub plane of the Cosmic Physical Plane of existence.
- The <u>second initiation</u> implies dominion over the Astral sub plane of the Cosmic Physical Plane of existence.
- The <u>third initiation</u> is passed when we have command over the Mental sub plane of the Cosmic Physical Plane of existence.
- The <u>fourth initiation</u> entails contact with and dominion over the Buddhic sub plane of the Cosmic Physical Plane of existence.
- The <u>fifth initiation</u> takes us to the Masters level by anchoring theAtmic sub plane of the Cosmic Physical Plane of existence. Passing this initiation, the individual attains entrance to the planetary hierarchy and terminates the cycles of planetary reincarnations.
- The <u>sixth initiation</u> conduce us to the Christ level and secures contact with the Monadic sub plane of the Cosmic Physical Plane of existence.
- The <u>seventh initiation</u> takes us to mastery of the Logoic sub plane of the Cosmic Physical Plane of existence.
- The <u>eighth and ninth</u> initiations conduce us to the levels of our Planetary Logos and Solar Logos respectively.

Once we complete the ninth initiation, we may abandon the Cosmic Physical Plane of existence and move on toward further advancement through the higher cosmic planes of existence by taking yet innumerable initiations. This path of initiations constitute our travelling back Home and back to our true spiritual nature and connection to the Divine. We must bring this awareness fully into our human condition.Then, we can attain freedom.

Each of the planetary initiations is forged by the energy of one or several of the Cosmic Rays of Creation, resulting in control of and power over the specific energies by the individual taking the initiation. The internal effects produced by these initiations on the individual taking them would be a tremendous invigoration of the energy centers or chakras (one at a time), with the resultant enlargement of their field of influence and full activation; whereas the external or purely physical effects will be the energizing of the nervous system as well as the pineal and pituitary glands.

<u>PLANETARY INITIATIONS</u>
<u>First Initiation: "The Birth"</u>

This denomination is a metaphor. It refers to a <u>spiritual birth</u>, to be born to a new way of life which is commanded purely by spirit. It represents the latent Christ that must be born within each one of us. It incriminates complete adjustment and total balance in the Physical sub plane of the Cosmic Physical Plane of existence. Thus it is an initiation related to dense matter that <u>corresponds with the sacred element earth, and its symbol is bread.</u> This initiation implies achieving <u>mastery over our physical body</u> and opening our eyes to focus far beyond the merely physical or material.

From the point of view of energy, <u>the principal chakra that is activated during this initiation is the</u>**First, Root or Base chakra**that represents a physical state of consciousness. Yet, the Second, Sacral or Polarity chakra that represents sexuality, creativity and primordial emotions, is also further invigorated and evolved, resulting in its energy rising toward the Fifth or Throat chakra that represents expression of creativity and will, thus allowing the concrete expression of the creativity force to show itself in a proper or positive manner.

Furthermore, the Fourth or Heart chakra that represents inclusive love is stimulated as a consequence of the dissolution of the heavy etheric sheet existing between the   and the Fourth or Heart chakra, due to the impetus of ascending energy from the First, Root or Base chakra. This occurrence prepares the individual for doing further work on the development of its astral or emotional body.

<u>The energy of the Seventh Cosmic Ray of Creation that represents ceremonial magic and order is the predominant energy influencing this initiation</u>. The energy of this Cosmic Ray of Creation is linked to creativity, manifestation and order, and it is the energy responsible for the conjunction of spirit and matter.

In order to achieve this first initiation, we must work on the purification of the physical body by overcoming harmful physical temptations and transmuting the lower basic physical inclinations. This work is done through paying attention to the diet (ingesting pure nutrients and water), movement, rest/sleep habits, proper attitude in sexual activity, manner of speech, periods of silence, contact with nature and working on the cleansing of the energy system. All of these would help in keeping the physical body free of toxin accumulation.

Thus this initiation encompasses the following subjects:

- Nutrition
- Health
- Survival
- Sexuality
- The material world and means of subsistence

The first steps should be directed to correct wrong perceptions about the physical body and the material world of existence, since they both act as external mirrors that are reflecting to us our inner condition. Also the external world around bring us important messages. This is the very reason why we should learn to embrace and accept the circumstances around us.

We must transform our physical body in terms of rendering it into the most pure and appropriate vehicle for spirit. We ought to bring spirituality to the body. The beginning point for us to do this is to maintain an attitude of acceptance and love toward the physical body. Then:

- We have to get deeply in touch with our physical body and learn to listen carefully to its messages.
- We must keep the body grounded and in intimate relation with mother earth.
- We must bring to perfect equilibrium our physical body and the surrounding material world.
- We have to acknowledge both the masculine and feminine natures in ourselves and balance them regardless of our gender by physical birth.
- We must learn to look at sex and money only as symbols of sharing and communicating with authentic care.
- We ought to learn to see the physical body as an instrument to express love and good in the world.

In this manner we can reach a physical level of consciousness that remains in a healthy balance. Our physical level of consciousness is represented by the energy of the First, Root or Base chakra which awakens and develops through this kind of work on ourselves.

If we entertain an exaggerated focus of attention on the physical body, we create imbalance in our being, as much as if we completely neglect it. If we are too much preoccupied and troubled we bring destruction to the physical body; while on the contrary, acceptance and love invigorates it.

When spirit is permitted to express through our physical level of consciousness (Root Chakra), our lives are changed into great experiences in both areas: our physical body and the material world around us. When this condition is reached, we feel joyful in our physical activities; have vitality and good health, a sense of deep purpose, material abundance and a beneficent environment.

Through the process for accomplishing this initiation we now have learnt certain lessons as follows:

- To have more command over our thoughts, speech and actions.
- To see more clearly and distinguish illusions (material world) from reality (spiritual world).
- To be less concerned with external things.
- More knowledge about electromagnetic fields and the interplay of different forces in the physical world.

Also, since this initiation stimulates the Heart Chakra it marks the awakening of a purer modality of love, a higher force that is capable of metamorphosing lust into love and selfish consciousness into group consciousness that implies understanding, harmony and responsibility toward other beings, including all kingdoms of nature.

The realization that the Christ consciousness begins to awaken within us brings the acceptance of the same consciousness that is also present in others and shifts our focus from the physical body toward the soul extension that now becomes our guidance. The lower energies that we have so ascended trigger response from our higher spiritual bodies in the form of descending light energy that reinforces the process of transformation.

In summary, passing the first initiation signs the beginning of a new way of living for the individual, characterized by a different and fresh perception of self and the world, a new way of thinking, and a novel attitude toward life and others. In order to attain this condition, the structure of the person should be able to hold and sustain 30% of pure light.

Span between the First and Second Initiations

The individual must continue the same spiritual work consciously, steadfastly and faithfully. He/she must begin to pay attention to mechanical emotional reactions that distort the true perception of things and should try to overcome them by the use of a clear mind to reason properly. The emotional body must be evolved toward a state of stable balance.

Second Initiation: "The Baptism"

This is a fluid initiation, thus its symbol is the sacred element water.It is the symbol representing the act of entering the river of spiritual life. It represents total involvement with spiritual growth and results in complete adjustment to and balance in the Astral sub plane of the Cosmic Physical Plane of existence. The main energy center that is stimulated in this initiation is the Second, Sacral or Polarity Chakra, nonetheless the that represents personal power is stimulated as well and this produces an upward movement of its desire energy toward the Fourth or Heart Chakra which holds the energy of all inclusive love. This happening renders the individual more responsive to the promptings of the soul and more loving toward humanity in general.

The rising energy dissolves the dense etheric web existing between the Fourth or Heart Chakra and the Fifth or Throat Chakra that represents will power and expression, allowing the later chakra to develop further.

The Cosmic Ray of Creation which energy is cardinal during this initiation is the Sixth Ray which stands for devotion, idealism and emotional order, and connects individuals to their higher objectives.

In order to achieve this initiation, we must work on the purification and evolvement of the emotional or astral body, thus our responsibility should be to attain emotional healing and mastery over the emotional body. The related matters we should pay attention to are:

- Our feelings.
- The quality of our emotions and our emotional reactions.
- Our desires.
- The quality of our relationships.
- Traumas of the past.
- The feminine energy within.
- The contents of our subconscious mind.

Feelings refer to the perception of: physical sensations, emotional sensations, desire sensations and mental states. Feelings encompass a broader field than emotions. Emotions are only the manifestation of the emotional body. Our more basic and restricted emotional behavior is rooted in both the Second or Sacral and the energy centers, while our expanded and higher emotions stem from the Fourth or Heart energy center which is in direct connection with the soul; thus experiences of love and joy originating at this level are very different from those that emerge from the lower emotional centers.

In reality, we can say that there exist only two emotions: love and fear. These two emotions each originate a group of their own, from the most exalted (happiness – joy – bliss) which depend on the original emotion of love, to the more basic ones (lust – anger – hatred) which depend on the original emotion of fear. We may also say that fear is the absence of love, and all the manifestations of fear such as aggressive behavior resulting in depression and isolation, may appear when love is not experienced.

The emotional aspect of humans, as the physical aspect, is largely influenced by the way they think. So emotions turn to be more an "effect" than a "cause" or creative force. However, especially when the person is not a master of its mind, both the physical and emotional aspects can also influence the mental body and the manner of thinking. But we must never forget that the three lower principles or bodies (physical – emotional – mental) are like antennas or sensors of the soul for its interaction with the environment and eventually should respond to the soul's directions.

Two kinds of emotions may produce great restrictions in the course of our lives, namely 1) Hostile and aggressive emotions which often make others the victims, such as anger and hatred; and 2) Passive emotions which mainly victimize us, such as suffering and resentment. On the other hand, the presence of emotions brings as well positive aspects as follows: Emotions represent our reactions to experiences either of love (union) or fear (isolation) and thus they mirror to us our state of consciousness. In a way, the emotions we experience are based on our beliefs and elections. We must learn to see and regard them only as indicators or flags that call our attention toward our own state of being and signal what must be corrected. Thus, emotions should not be permitted to rule over us and dictate our actions.

In order to comprehend the true function of the emotional principle and work on the purification of this body we should:

- First of all we ought to face our emotions, get in touch with them, do not run away from them, do not repress them and learn to look at them as a sort of guidance for us to work on ourselves; knowing that they are but energy currents in motion and so eventually they will run their course and disappear.
- We must direct our work toward the cleansing and harmonizing of the emotional body, for which purpose we should discover both our emotional weaknesses and strengths. What we call "negative emotions" are only signals of emotional disharmony and commotion. Therefore we must learn how to bring about a calm state to this emotional nature of ours.
- We must work with our mind toward this end of peace by removing the influence of false and harmful beliefs over the emotional nature.
- We must fully acknowledge the feminine nature in human beings, disregarding gender.
- We must develop latent positive qualities as well as encourage the ones already showing up openly in our personality make up.
- We must encourage the practice of service to others.
- The practice of positive affirmations and visualization could help greatly in doing this work. For instance, imagining ourselves as the equivalent to a very peaceful mass of pure water, or simply visualizing the image of a beautifully calm lake. This would contribute to allow the emotional body to remain still and overcome the mood swings that continually appear and disappear.
- The practice of meditation produces the same pacifying effect.
- Further help may be provided by hypnotherapy and regression therapy.

In order to achieve this initiation, the individual must know how to be above the selfish desires of the lower personality, closer to the higher purpose of the soul, and how to reach a state of emotional equilibrium that will be reflected by a totally purified emotional principle.

This initiation brings about a deeper knowledge of the Astral plane of existence and the workings of the Universal Law of Karma, or Law of Cause and Effect. By the time an individual attains this initiation he/she has learned the following:

- To answer with an attitude of equanimity in the face of opposites.
- To regard emotions only for what they truly are and not to give them power to rule.
- To conquer any state of doubt.
- To move the focus of attention toward the mental body in order to give the mind power over negative emotional reactions.

The final results after achieving this initiation are:

- The person becomes more aware of the existence of the soul, which is the messenger of higher spiritual bodies.
- The individual senses the true links of unity with others and perceives the self as part of a whole that shares the same higher ideals and goals.

- He/she can remain steady in the practice of deep meditation.
- The desire to serve humanity is but mandatory now.
- The loving capacity expands to cover all of creation.
- The individual has mastered the emotional body.

In order to pass this initiation the human being's structure must be able to hold 40% of pure light.

Span between the Second and Third Initiations

The person must continue working on the purification of the emotional body by means of using the lower mind and meditation practice. He/she increasingly moves away from selfish personal interests to considering more the interest of the whole, hence encouraging further the attitude of service and the lower mind (intellect) turns more and more under the guidance of the soul extension, the individual begins to learn a great deal about the Mental Plane of existence and the role of thought in the act of creation.

Third Initiation: "The Transfiguration"

This is a mental initiation, it is a baptism of fire, thus fire is its symbol. It is about acquiring mastery of the mental body, integrating and coordinating the three lower bodies and merging with the energy of the soul extension. Now the individual is adjusted to and balanced in the Mental Sub plane of the Cosmic Physical Plane of existence and attains complete control over the physical world and his/her human personality. The three lower bodies increment notoriously its overall vibratory frequency and the personality becomes totally responsive to the guidance of the soul. Then, as a consequence the person is principally focused on the soul extension and the Mental Plane of existence.

The energy center that becomes more stimulated during this initiation is the
that represents the energy of personal power and the state of human consciousness. In addition, the Sixth or Third Eye Chakra that holds the energy of inner vision and intuition becomes completely developed. Due to the ascending motion of energy, the etheric web between the Fifth or Throat Chakra and the Sixth or Third Eye Chakra dissolves and the Seventh or Crown Chakra is as well further activated.

During this initiation the main influence comes from the energy of the Fifth Cosmic Ray of Creation, ray of concrete mind and science which eventually will uncover the door that conduces to reach the state of "Universal Mind."
Our personal work in the pursue of attaining this initiation involves the complete purification and dominion of the lower mental body and the pertinent issues are:

- Intellectual development which includes studying and exercising the faculty of reasoning.
- Firm determination and the use of will power.
- Organization power and the use of focus and concentration. The lower mind must be trained to focus and to direct action, but in equal measure it should be trained to quiet down and remain receptive to the energy of the heart, as well as to insights and inspiration arising from the higher realms. When the lower mind surrenders to spirit's guidance it becomes truly expanded and unlimited.
- Slowing down the erratic activity of the mind.

- Mastery of thought and mind power, always keeping a positive attitude. The individual must become liberated from its own habitual deleterious thought patterns as well as from the influence of the mass consciousness of humanity.
- Exercising the capacity for right discrimination and choice.

The human lower mind is, generally speaking, the kingdom of the ego; nevertheless, its faculties have the possibility of being developed and advanced to a point where the individual begins to use them with a higher purpose than that of personal aggrandizement. In these cases the mind is guided by spirit and the person's triumph consists in the complete elimination of the "individual personality consciousness" that continually manipulates and demands. The fact that we must focus our work on the lower mind at this stage of growth in no way means that we should neglect the physical and emotional aspects of our being.

So, in order to accomplish mastery over the lower mental body, we must:

- Eliminate some customary thought patterns that are detrimental to our spiritual growth. Most of these are inherited from our parents and society, thus we must turn free from previous conditioning of the mind.
- In consequence, we must re-program our lower mind with a healthy, positive and spiritual tendency.
- Become acutely aware of all our negative thoughts that poison us and pollute the mental atmosphere of our surroundings, thus we must work toward its cleansing and purification.
- Encourage the development of a thinking process that accepts and blesses every circumstance of life rather than resisting, protesting and cursing.
- Become clearly aware of all our selfish thoughts and work for the favorable transformation of this modality.
- Realize that our thoughts should not be repressed or denied, but observed. Then we can focus on working for the purification and transformation of our mental body, which will bring about clearer and luminous thought forms that will be aligned with the Divine Plan.
- Orient our mind toward the planning of service activity.
- Learn to correct false perceptions of self, others and surrounding reality. We can do this if first of all we accept the spiritual world, change false beliefs (since thoughts creates reality), and end the sense of duality.
- Practice using positive affirmations and visualization, for these help to create the custom of positive thinking as well as to re-program both conscious and subconscious parts of the mind. These new ways, in turn, will influence beneficially our emotions and actions.
- Practice meditation since this is extremely helpful for quieting the lower mind in order to allow access to higher consciousness. Also, through meditation, we can develop the mental bridge existing between our lower and higher minds, which eventually results in purely divine energy descending from our spiritual bodies to saturate the lower ones.
- The use of aids such as Hypnotherapy and Regression therapy is also helpful.

The overall requirement to accomplish this initiation is to conquer mental temptations, arrogance and pride. The individual acquires deep knowledge about and understanding of the following:

- The Mental Plane of existence.
- The role of energy as encountered in matter, in individual human beings, and in groups of persons.
- The energy represented by the Third Cosmic Ray of creation or the third divine aspect of Active Intelligence.
- The functioning of our solar system.
- Our planet Earth and the lower kingdoms of nature.
- The evolutionary process of creation.
- The Law of Polarity.
- The underlying oneness of creation.

Reaching this initiation implies that the person has already learned:

- To reach and sustain a state of equanimity or subjugation of both the states of attraction (desiring) and rejection.
- To overthrow mental illusions, that is, knowing with certainty what is true.
- The correct use of choice or knowing what is good and right for spiritual evolution.
- The correct use of the lower mind (intellect) which entails allowing the soul extension to use and direct the mental body.
- Perfect knowledge of when, at will, to quiet the mind or focus it in order to direct a necessary action. This is the true mastery of the lower mind.
- Concrete expression and use of psychic abilities (clairvoyance – clairaudience – clairsentience – telepathy – etc.) for the benefit of humanity and all creation.

At this point in the spiritual growth of a person, the energy of that person's Monad has a direct repercussion on the spiritual bodies and soul extension. Consequently the personality or the three lower bodies is immersed in light, expressing itself as all-inclusive love and desire to serve for the good of a whole, and for the advancement of the Divine Plan of creation. There is no more sense of disunion, nor false attraction by matter, nor judgments of any kind. Wisdom and love are blended and the person is absolutely conscious of his/her multidimensional nature, acting as such. Thus the results are:

- The individual is now detached from the attraction of dense matter
- The individual exhibits less necessity for food and sleep to remain physically alive.
- The individual lives through compassion, only to help others.
- The individual has mastered the laws governing the process of creative thought building. Therefore the individual is now capable of producing the concrete manifestation of his/her thoughts.

From the point of view of energy movements, what happens during the third initiation is as follows: The person, through the development of the mental bridge of energy, has learned to focus conscious attention on the Monad (original spark of spirit), and this persistent focus can attract the powerful monadic energy toward the personality. This descending energy contains divine masculine (+) and feminine (-) forces; the female energy spiraling down in a clockwise motion, enveloping the physical body to its base and then ascending through the spinal cord up to the Fourth or Heart Chakra where it encounters the male energy that has descended in a counterclockwise spiral motion (inside the female energy) and entered the body through the Seventh or Crown Chakra. This encounter and merger of energies represents the true "Birth of the Christ Consciousness" in the individual. Then the female divine energy from the Monad continue ascending through the spinal cord and the male divine energy keeps descending through the Crown Chakra until they meet once more at the level of the Sixth or Third Eye Chakra.

The person who passes the third initiation is then capable of consciously stepping down the powerful monadic energy, controlling it, directing it, and projecting it outward through the Third Eye Chakra. This makes him/her a conscious creator within the Physical Plane of existence and is what we call "The Transfiguration," for which the person needs approximately 56% of light energy held within its being.

FIGURE #1

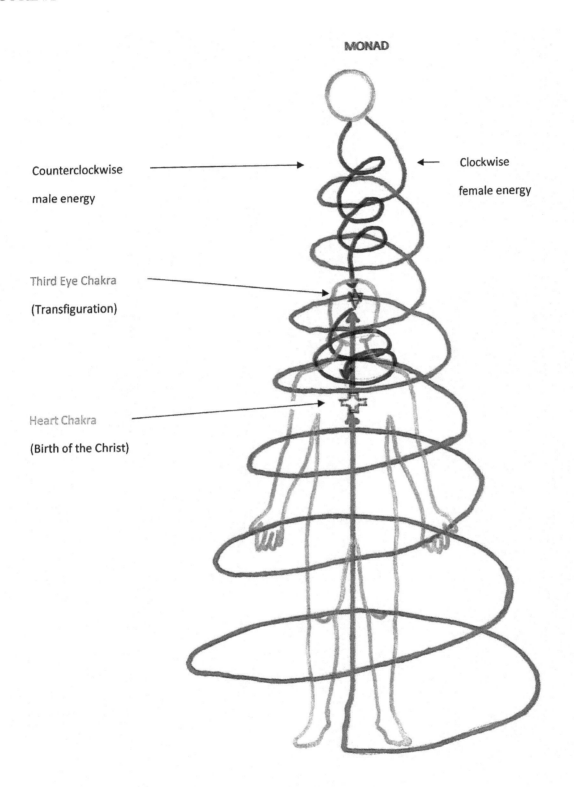

The first three initiations (Birth – Baptism – Transfiguration), considered together, represent concrete expressions of the energy of the   ; therefore the different challenges to be faced in achieving them are all related to distinct aspects of knowledge and experiences leading the individual toward the state of group consciousness.

Span between the Third and Fourth Initiations

From this point on, the process of spiritual growth, with its inherent expansion of consciousness, unfolds rapidly. The individual leads a life of meditation and service to humanity guided by a clear mind, love and group consciousness. The person steps down, receives, moderates, directs and projects energy from the spiritual bodies to the manifested external world. He/she continues learning, especially about the Buddhic Plane of existence and the work of the "building Divas of nature" that follow the law of attraction and love.

Fourth Initiation: "The Crucifixion" or "The Great Renunciation"

This is an intuitive initiation of air which is its symbol, as well as the cross. It implies some kind of sacrifice (that in reality is only an apparent sacrifice), and liberation from the material world by laying down all attachments and demonstrating absolute faith in spirit. The person becomes adjusted to and balanced in the Buddhic subplane of the Cosmic Physical Plane of existence.

The energy center becoming totally developed during this initiation is the Fourth or Heart Chakra that represents unconditional love energy and the dense etheric disc between the Sixth or Third Eye Chakra and the Seventh or Crown Chakra disintegrates. The cosmic ray of creation associated to this initiation is Cosmic Ray Four that carries the energy of struggle to finally reach harmony and beauty. This energy originates internal and external conflicts which we must endure until we learn to choose harmony.

The personal work required to pass this initiation encompasses the following:

- The expansion of compassion and development of unlimited love toward humanity.
- Extending love to animals, plants and the planet itself.
- Developing a sense of oneness with all creation.
- The practice of acceptance and forgiveness.
- The encouragement of living in joy.
- Expanding the use of imagination and creativity.
- Learning to completely let go and surrender to a higher power.
- Learning to relate and integrate all our experiences which is the way of learning through the heart and not through the head. Ultimately, we need to make our life decisions from this heart center which is the seat of the soul extension.

This personal spiritual work leads to the termination of the need and desire to live within a physical form in a sense of isolation from the whole. This is now what the individual renounces to.

Taking into account the movement of energy, the individual who has accomplished this initiation has totally purified and integrated the three lower chakras. Therefore the energy moves and ascends as follows:

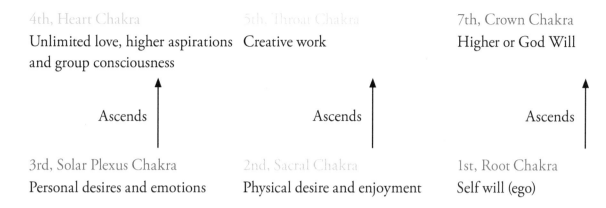

4th, Heart Chakra
Unlimited love, higher aspirations and group consciousness

5th, Throat Chakra
Creative work

7th, Crown Chakra
Higher or God Will

Ascends

Ascends

Ascends

3rd, Solar Plexus Chakra
Personal desires and emotions

2nd, Sacral Chakra
Physical desire and enjoyment

1st, Root Chakra
Self will (ego)

This initiation signals the commencement of the blending of the higher spiritual bodies of the individual and his/her Monad. At this stage, the individual's personality (three lower bodies) is functioning totally under the direction of the soul extension in an absolute and indelible manner. The person is, as well, sustaining a conscious focus of attention on the higher spiritual bodies.

During this initiation the person receives information related to:

- The veritable nature and purpose of learning through duality and the balance that must be achieved between two apparently opposed forces within the Law of Polarity or Law of Pendulum.
- Also, there is further learning about the purpose of relationships in general and all that pertains to the second divine aspect represented by the Cosmic Ray II of Creation (Love/Wisdom), such as the secret of building forms or structures by using the energy of love or attraction.
- The functioning of our solar system within our galaxy and its center.
- Further knowledge about the parallel evolutions, besides the human, in our planetary system: angelic and devic.
- Information about the Buddhic and Atmic sub planes of the Physical Cosmic plane of existence.

At this point of personal growth, individuals experience a sense of loss and hopelessness, as well as a sense that all aspects of life as they know it seem to be falling apart and dying. Persons and things that acted as external supports and to which the individual was attached no longer provide the usual contentment and gratification, or they are literally taken away from the person. The individual now has no other relationships but with Self, Teachers and God. He/she has let go all material attachments as well as the former lower-self. The person is experiencing existence only through the point of view of the spiritual bodies and the Monad, since he/she has merged completely with these bodies that are expressions of the Monad, which now becomes the unique source of guidance.

At the completion of this initiation the person has learned:

- Total detachment.
- All inclusive love and sharing.
- Complete assimilation and integration of all life experiences and learning.

When this initiation is attained, the outcome is as follows:

- The person has become a master of compassion and wisdom, with power over the three lower levels of existence (physical – astral – lower mental) and with universal awareness.
- The individual has totally balanced personal as well as group karmic forces.
- The sole preoccupation of the person is to assist the planet and humanity.
- The individual has ended the need for reincarnation in his/her personal evolution, wherefore there is no further necessity for a personality (three lower bodies) to manifest, and consequently freedom and liberation are attained.
- This initiation depicts the movement from the fourth kingdom of nature (Human) to the fifth kingdom or Soul kingdom.
- The person can now work from a higher level of existence (the Buddhic plane of consciousness) in order to contribute to the evolution of the planet and humanity in general.
- To remain involved in the material world of existence becomes now a voluntary decision to serve at this level, as it is also the decision to return in order to accomplish further initiations while incarnated in a physical body.
- For this initiation to take place, the person's structure should be capable of holding 62% of pure light.

Span between the Fourth and Fifth Initiations

The individual has become part of the Fifth Kingdom of Souls and of the Planetary Hierarchy, so the expansion of his/her consciousness is now faster. There may be a voluntary return to the three lower worlds of existence with the purpose of reaffirming what was already accomplished, or the purpose to continue taking initiations from this level of existence, or the purpose to teach and serve humanity in its advancement.

Otherwise, the new master works ceaselessly from the Buddhic plane of existence for the good of humanity and the whole of creation, as well as teaching to soul groups. He/ she has the power to manifest at will a body that resembles the human one, if need comes to contact incarnated individuals. Also, there is further learning for him/her about the role of light and sound in creation.

Fifth Initiation: "The Revelation"

This planetary initiation is also considered as the first cosmic initiation. It is a <u>spiritual initiation which symbol is ether</u>. The individual becomes <u>adjusted and balanced to the Atmic sub-plane of the Cosmic Physical plane of existence. The energy center that is totally expanded in this initiation is the</u> Fifth or Throat Chakra which represents expression of the will. In addition, the First or Root Chakra is energized. The <u>Cosmic Ray involved now is **Ray I of Will and Purpose of God**</u> and this energy compels the individual to find the true significance of the highest aspect of Divine Will which encompasses:

- The correct use of the will power in manifestation.
- The will for good, always.
- The working of the "demolishing" aspect of divinity.

The necessary work to achieve this initiation is related to:

- Meditation and prayer.
- Wholeness.
- Acceptance, integration and balance.

- Development of divine vision and divine will.

The main challenge of this initiation is to be correct in the interpretation of revelations. This initiation implies complete merger with the divine Self, the Monad and the person remembers itself as such. The individual will receive information and revelations about the following:

- The Cosmic Rays of creation.
- The energy of our Solar System and the relation to its center.
- The purpose of the Planetary Logos.
- The purpose and meaning of life in the three lower planes of existence (physical – astral – mental).
- The next stages on the path of higher evolution.
- The Monadic Plane of existence.

When this initiation is completed the individual would have learned:

- To see everything and to think as God.

At this stage in personal evolution, the individual (Master) has achieved in consciousness a complete fusion and unification of the different parts of its constitution, namely Monad/Spiritual bodies/ Soul/ dominated personality. As a result of this we have the following:

- The individual is functioning from the levels of higher mind (abstract mind), intuitive love/wisdom (Buddhi aspect), and spiritual will (Atmic aspect), all of which corresponds to the spiritual bodies.
- The person is openly and consciously connected to the Planetary Hierarchy.
- The Master originates new ideas and designs for service to the Divine Plan at different levels of creation.
- The Master has direct access to the whole planetary energy, including all the kingdoms of nature (Mineral – Vegetal – Animal – Human) and also the parallel lines of energy involved in planet Earth's evolution (Elemental evolution – Angelic energies).
- The Master exists in a state of unbroken continuity of consciousness; that is, with complete awareness of his/her multidimensional existence and innumerable incarnations.
- This initiation requires the individual to be able to hold 75% of pure light within its structure.

Span between the Fifth and Sixth Initiations

This period involves further work to learn about and use rightly the attribute of Divine Will. Also, the formation of working groups around the Master.

Sixth Initiation: "The Decision"

This planetary initiation is considered as well as the second cosmic initiation. It is related to the resolution the individual must make, either to remain working for the advancement of planet Earth, or move beyond to the paths of higher evolution such as Solar and Cosmic evolution.

The sixth initiation involves adjustment to and balance in the Monadic sub plane of the Cosmic Physical plane of existence, being its symbol light. The main energy centers to be totally activated are the Sixth or Third Eye Chakra which is involved with spiritual vision and the Fifth or Throat Chakra involved with creative expression.

During this initiation, the individual shall merge totally and actually with its Monad, not only in consciousness. The mental bridge of light linking the lower and higher bodies has been fully developed; allowing the monadic energy to infuse unimpeded the soul and personality (three lower bodies) which becomes pure light. This is what has been called "a completed planetary ascension" and the person thus becomes an

Ascended Master. For a person to turn into a clear and pure vessel for the expression of spirit (Monad), all vestiges of impurity must be vanished and all work remaining must be that of service.

The <u>principal energy</u> provided for this initiation from the Cosmic Rays of Creation is that of which represents the Third Divine Aspect. The necessary work to accomplish this initiation is related to:

- Sustained introspection and meditation.
- Enduring the integration of all planetary lives and all the achieved learning with the true divine condition of the human being.
- Becoming a pure and complete manifestation of inner peace and wisdom.
- The continuous calling forth of love and light.
- Having a permanent "unified vision" or the perception of absolute oneness.
- Enduring expression of all inclusive love and joy.

At this point the main lesson learned is about manifesting love and light; and the main challenge has been to learn how to make correct decisions or the development of right discernment. The results emerging out of the completion of this initiation are:

- Perfect understanding of the creative process, the essence of creation and the meaning of manifestation in different forms of substance.
- Mastery and power at all levels of planetary life.
- Permanent state of love and acceptance for all creation.
- God consciousness.

For this initiation to be completed, the individual's structure must be capable of holding 80% of pure light. As a result, the light energy of the Monad descends through the mental bridge (Antahkarana) and inundates the lower bodies transmuting them into pure light. This includes the physical body which then becomes the so called "light body." Thus, this "light body" is built upon the light which the individual has acquired all throughout its incarnations.

The group constituted by the fourth, fifth and sixth initiations (Crucifixion – Revelation – Decision) depict expressions of the Second Divine Aspect or the energy of the Second Cosmic Ray of Creation (Love/Wisdom), so their challenges are linked to varied aspects of compassion, devotion, forgiveness, all inclusive love and service.

<u>Span between the Sixth and Seventh Initiations</u>

The Ascended Master now merges its will with that of the Planetary Logos and is guided by the most elevated center of the Planetary Hierarchy. There is further learning about the relation between the Planetary Logos and the Solar system, as well as about the divine intention of creators.

<u>Seventh Initiation: "The Resurrection"</u>

The true meaning of resurrection is: Return to a pristine or original state; that is, return to where we came from. The person goes back permanently to its monadic state.

This initiation consists of complete adjustment and balance in the Logoic sub plane of the Cosmic Physical Plane of existence. Therefore the individual's will has totally melded with the Planetary Logos will. The symbol of this particular initiation is spirit, and the main energy center that is fully activated is the Seventh or Crown Chakra. The Fourth or Heart Chakra is also fully energized and all the energy centers or chakras appear now as a single pillar of light that is connected to the ascension bridge Antahkarana. The energy of Cosmic Ray II of Creation (Love/Wisdom) is the main directive of this initiation.

The work required for the completion of this initiation is related to:

- Full activation and manifestation of the First Divine Aspect or the energy of Cosmic Ray I of Creation (Spiritual Will/ Power/ Purpose).
- Full activation and manifestation of the Second Divine Aspect or the energy of Cosmic Ray II of Creation (Spiritual Love/Wisdom).

The challenge at this point is to learn to combine and perfectly blend the manifestation of the First and Second Divine Aspects with the sole and unique orientation toward service to the Divine Plan of Creation. The individual receives advanced knowledge about the veritable essence of Cosmic Ray II energy (Love/Wisdom) and the workings of the "attraction force," as well as further revelation about the whole Solar System and its Logos.

The results pertaining to the completion of this initiation are:

- Consistent state of liberation and complete planetary ascension.
- Full mastery of the seven sub planes of the Cosmic Physical Plane of existence and of the seven Cosmic Rays of Creation. Thus the individual is prepared to move out and beyond the Cosmic Physical Plane of existence and continue its evolutionary path on the way to cosmic ascension (total of 352 levels of initiation).
- The beginning of advancement beyond all physical laws.
- Becoming a focal point of pure light.
- Permanent relinquishment of ego negativity.
- Permanent and total dedication to service, guidance and teaching.

At the completion of this initiation, the personal structure of the individual should be ready to hold 92% of pure light. This is the highest initiation to be taken in this earthly plane of existence. Nonetheless, there are still two more initiations that can be taken in an ascended state of existence. These nine levels of initiation correspond to the seven sub planes of the Cosmic Physical Plane of existence, which individuals can leave behind once they surmount the ninth initiation. However, the Ascended Master shall return to the place from where he/she ascended, with the purpose of bringing "Heaven to Earth." That is, to correctly demonstrate all spiritual learning in daily practical life and offer the gifts of spirit to all, for the advancement of the most possible peoples of the world. Such will be a life without any struggles, based solely on insights, inspiration, service and teaching at all levels: during wake, meditation and sleeping times; a life of uninterrupted activity and in a state of continuity of consciousness.

Eighth Initiation: "The Transition"

This initiation implies further involvement with and growth of planetary consciousness. The Ascended Master receives more knowledge about the purpose and aim of planetary life as well as new information about the workings of duality at this level and the nature of the solar system.

For this initiation, the combined energies of cosmic rays IV (Harmony through conflict), V (Science), VI (Devotion) and VII (Ceremonial magic) exert their influence. The structure of the individual must be able to hold 96% of pure light.

Span between the Eighth and Ninth Initiations

At this point, if the individual has already chosen to continue its service to planet Earth and humanity, she/he persevere working toward this end. This decision was made during the Sixth Initiation. On the contrary, if the person has chosen otherwise, he/she may advance to the following initiation and consequently to the higher paths of spiritual evolution through the remaining Cosmic Planes of manifestation. These are the paths of Cosmic Evolution.

Ninth Initiation: "The Refusal"

This initiation implies the reaffirmation of declining the option of continuing the service to planet Earth. The Ascended Master now exists solely at a Monadic level of universal awareness, expressing purely the first three Divine Attributes of Love/Wisdom Will/Power and being a co-creator within the energy of its Cosmic Ray. The Master is the depositary of new revelations about creation and the Solar Logos.

The Cosmic Ray's energies involved in this initiation are those of **Ray I (Will/Purpose of God**, Ray II (Love/Wisdom of God, and .The structure of the Master now holds 100% of pure light.

The seventh, eighth and ninth initiations, together as a group, typify the energy of the First Divine Aspect or Cosmic Ray I of Will/Purpose of God. Therefore all the challenges facing the individual are related to the correct use of all the aspects of will. It is also important to mention that as human beings go through the process of evolution and initiations, so does planet Earth and its Logos (spirit embedding the planet).

Table #2

	1st Initiation	**2nd Initiation**	**3rd Initiation**
Name:	"The Birth"	"The Baptism"	"The Transfiguration"
Symbol:	Earth/Bread	Water	Fire
Chakra stimulated:	Root CH.	Sacral CH.	
Cosmic Ray energy:	Ray VII Ceremonial order and Magic	Ray VI Emotional order and Devotion	Ray V Concrete mind and Science
Necessary work:	Purification of the Physical body.	Purification of the Emotional body.	Purification of the Lower Mental body.
Results:	Mastery over the physical body, speech and actions.	Mastery of the emotional body. Expansion of the capacity to love and service others.	Mastery of the mental body. Correct choice and discrimination. Quieting the mind at will. The mind surrenders to the guidance of spirit.
Pure light held:	30%	40%	56%

Expressions of the Second Divine Aspect or Cosmic Ray II of Creation
Love/Wisdom

	4th Initiation	5th Initiation	6th Initiation
Name:	"The Crucifixion"	"The Revelation"	"The Decision"
Symbol:	Air/The Cross	Ether	Light
Chakra stimulated:	Heart CH.	Throat CH.	Third Eye CH.
Cosmic Ray energy:	Ray IV	Ray I	
	Harmony/Beauty	Will/Purpose	
Necessary work:	Develop all inclusive love, a sense of oneness, joy of living and creativity.	Develop divine will, purpose and vision. Total integration and balance.	Develop correct discernment. Manifestation of love, light and wisdom. Achieving enduring integration of all lives. Develop perception of absolute oneness.
Results:	Total detachment from physical matter. Integration of all experiences and learning. Mastery of physical, emotional and mental levels. Total balance of karma. Movement to the 5th Kingdom of Souls. End of the need for reincarnation.	Total wholeness. Merger with the Monad, in consciousness.	Completed planetary ascension. Perfect understanding of the creative process. Mastery of all planetary levels. God consciousness.
Pure light held:	62%	75%	80%

Expressions of the First Divine Aspect or Ray I of Creation
Will Power/Purpose

	7th Initiation	8th Initiation	9th Initiation
Name:	"The Resurrection"	"The Transition"	"The Refusal"
Symbol:	Spirit	Spirit	Spirit
Chakra stimulated:	Crown CH.		
Cosmic Ray energy:	Ray II	Rays IV, V, VI and VII	Rays I, II and
	Love/Wisdom	Harmony/Beauty	Will /Purpose
		Concrete mind/Science	Love/Wisdom
		Idealism/Devotion	
		Ceremonial magic	
Necessary work:	Full manifestation of the 1st and 2nd divine aspects and service to the Divine Plan.	Further growth of planetary consciousness.	Growth of universal consciousness.
Results:	Full mastery of the 7 rays and the 7 sub-planes of the Cosmic Physical Plane. Actual merger with the Monad. Merger with the Will of the Planetary Logos. State of liberation.	Full knowledge of the meaning and working of the Solar System and planetary life in duality.	Full expression of the 1st 3 divine aspects. Becoming a cocreator with God.
Pure light held:	92%	96%	100%

SYNTHESIS

- During the process of conscious spiritual work, human beings pass through progressive initiations and so does our planet Earth.

- An initiation marks the completion of a cycle of learning, challenges, and practical demonstration of that which was learned. Thus, each initiation is accompanied by progressive states of consciousness expansion.

- Initiations denote increasing levels of purification, unification of the human principles, and integration of pure light.

- Initiations are taken along a large span of planetary lives or reincarnations.

- Through the process of initiations, human beings ascend from the 4th kingdom of nature (Human kingdom) to the 5th kingdom of souls (Spirit kingdom) at the Hierarchy level of our planet.

- Nine initiations can be taken on the spiritual path within our system. Seven of them can be taken on the plane of our planet Earth and two can be taken as already ascended individuals. These seven planetary initiations are related to the seven sub-planes of the Cosmic Physical Plane of existence.

- 1st Initiation "The Birth": It refers to the birth of a new spiritual life (a purer form of life) and represents attunement to the Physical sub-plane of the Cosmic Physical Plane of existence. It is symbolized by "earth" and "bread" and it implies achieving mastery over the physical body through its full purification. The main chakra developed is the Root Chakra (Physical state of consciousness) and the main Cosmic Ray of Creation involved is Ray VII which is linked to creativity, manifestation, order and conjunction of spirit and matter. It signifies an increase of the pure light quotient, held within the structure of the individual, to 30%.

- 2nd Initiation "The Baptism": This refers to the act of entering the "river of spiritual life." It represents attunement to the Astral sub-plane of the Cosmic Physical Plane of existence. Its symbol is "water" and it involves achieving purification and mastery over the emotional body (emotional healing). It renders the individual more responsive to the soul energy and more loving toward humanity in general. The main chakra that expands is the Sacral or Polarity Chakra (emotional state of consciousness) and the principal influence is exerted by Cosmic Ray VI of Creation, which is related to idealism, devotion and emotional order. The quotient of pure light held increases to 40%.

- 3rd Initiation "The Transfiguration" : This refers to the transformation achieved through the complete integration and coordination of the three lower bodies with the soul and a direct contact with the Monad. It is a "baptism of fire." The personality becomes literally immersed in light and the individual becomes a conscious creator within the physical plane of existence. It represents attunement to the Mental sub-plane of the Cosmic Physical Plane of existence. Its symbol is "fire" and it implies purification and mastery of the lower mental body by moving away from the ego demands and learning to quiet the mind at will, as well as render it receptive to insights from the higher realms. The individual has complete control over the whole personality (three lower bodies) and follows the guidance of the soul. The expands (personal power and human consciousness) and the main influence comes from Cosmic Ray V of Creation which is involved with concrete mind and science. The quotient of pure light held augments to 56%.

- The 1st, 2nd and 3rd initiations together represent expressions of the 3rd Divine Aspect or (Active Intelligence and Manifestation). They are related to different aspects of knowledge that conduce the individual toward awakening consciousness to what we call "group consciousness," as opposed to "individual consciousness."

- 4<u>th</u> Initiation "The Crucifixion" : It implies an apparent sacrifice and liberation from the material world. It marks the movement from the 4<u>th</u> kingdom to the 5<u>th</u> kingdom. It represents attunement to Buddhic sub-plane of the Cosmic Physical Plane of existence. Its symbols are "air" and the "cross." The Heart Chakra expands and the Cosmic Ray involved in this initiation is Ray IV which deals with harmony and beauty. The individual has totally purified the energies of the three lower chakras as well as totally integrated all experiences of life. The capacity to love has expanded completely to the state of "all inclusive love" for all the kingdoms of nature, and there is a sense of oneness with all creation. It is the beginning of blending the higher spiritual bodies with the Monad. It implies mastery of material detachment, compassion and wisdom; as well as the end of karmic debts. The needed quotient of pure light is 62%.

- 5<u>th</u> Initiation "The Revelation" : It implies the realization of seeing oneself as the Monad (spark of pure spirit). There is attunement to the Atmic sub-plane of the Cosmic Physical Plane of existence. The symbol is "ether," the chakra developing fully is the 5<u>th</u> or Throat Chakra and the Cosmic Ray of Creation involved is Ray I of Will power/Purpose. The individual masters the proper use of Divine Vision and Will. There is fusion with the Monad, in consciousness. There is continuity of consciousness and direct connection to the Planetary Hierarchy. The required quotient of pure light is 75%.

- 6<u>th</u> Initiation "The Decision" : It refers to the choice either to remain working for the advancement of planet Earth or to continue further on the paths of higher evolution. It implies attunement to the Monadic sub-plane of the Cosmic Physical Plane of existence and its symbol is "light." The Third Eye Chakra develops fully and the energy of Cosmic   of Active Intelligence is involved. There is actual merger with the Monad and the individual completes planetary ascension, achieving mastery over all levels of planetary life. The quotient of pure light held is now 80%.

- The 4<u>th</u>, 5<u>th</u> and 6<u>th</u> initiations are expressions of the Second Divine Aspect or Cosmic Ray II (Love/ Wisdom of God).

- 7<u>th</u> Initiation "The Resurrection" : It implies the return to the pristine, original state or monadic state. There is attunement to the Logoic sub-plane of the Cosmic Physical Plane of existence. It implies merger with the Planetary Logos' Will and its symbol is "spirit." The main chakra to be activated is the Crown Chakra and the Cosmic Ray's influence is that of Ray II Love/Wisdom). There is mastery of all the seven sub-planes of the Cosmic Physical Plane of existence as well as mastery of the energies of the seven Cosmic Rays of Creation. The quotient of pure light held is 92%. This is the highest initiation that can be taken on the earthly plane.

- 8<u>th</u> Initiation "The Transition" : It implies extensive development of planetary consciousness. It is influenced by the combined energies of Cosmic Rays of Creation IV, V, VI and VII (Harmony/ Beauty – Concrete mind/Science – Idealism/Devotion – Ceremonial order/Magic). The quotient of pure light held is 96%.

- 9<u>th</u> Initiation "The Refusal" : It means the actual refusal to continue serving planet Earth. There is mastery of the first three Divine Attributes (Rays I, II and   ) and the individual exists at a Monadic level as a co-creator. The energies of Cosmic Rays of Creation I, II and   influence this initiation and the quotient of pure light held is 100%.

- Initiations 7<u>th</u>, 8<u>th</u> and 9<u>th</u> all express the energy of the First Divine Aspect or Cosmic Ray I (Will/ Purpose/Power of God).

CHAPTER VII

SUMMARIES
<u>SUMMARY OF STAGES OF AWAKENING OF CONSCIOUSNESS</u>

<u>Early Stage</u>

This human stage is closer to the third kingdom of nature or animal kingdom. The focus of attention is on survival, basically on the external world and on satisfying physical needs. The physical body represents the principal energy of influence over the individual.

The person has completely forgotten its source and true nature and thus lives a life of illusions, fed solely with the information provided by the physical senses. This is a condition characterized by ignorance and suffering, where the mind remains in a kind of latent state.

In this state of individuality and separation, the person experiences only a sense of self-consciousness of vitality and is not cognizant of the soul's presence nor has any conflicts of consciousness. The energies that rule the individual's life are, in order of importance: At the foremost, the energy of the Cosmic Ray overshadowing the physical body; then the energy of the Cosmic Ray of the emotional body of the person, and last the energy of the Cosmic Ray ruling the lower mental body.

<u>Middle Stage</u>

At this stage, a sense of conflict and duality commences to be felt by the person, the result of the soul extension being tugged on one side by the physical body's energy and on the other by spirit. So these two polarities begin a sort of war that is really happening between the inner and outer aspects of the individual. This situation, in truth, will permit the development of the lower mind through exerting the latent capacities of discrimination and choice.

This stage marks the awakening to a yet dim sense about the existence of the soul and the beginning of the necessary process of purification and cleansing by getting away with the dense layers enveloping the central light essence of the individual. A new energy begins to rise and become more predominant over the energies of the Cosmic Rays ruling each of the three lower bodies. This is the energy of the Cosmic Ray that rules the coordinated personality of the individual. As a consequence, the individual becomes more confident and can fully express his/her personality, although at this point the goals of the person are still very personal and materialistically oriented.

This stage is the beginning point for the amplification and demonstration of the Third Divine Aspect or the energy of   . This development will eventually lead to the total submission of sensory perceptions and intellect to the higher mind aspect of the individual (Manas).

<u>Advanced Stage</u>

At this level the person moves its focus of attention and identification from the lower bodies toward the soul extension, and begins to transit the bridge that links the 4th or Human Kingdom of nature and the 5th or Soul Kingdom.

Little by little, the individual moves away from the promptings of the ego personality and turns more sensitive to the collective needs of humanity, following higher ideals and looking at an exalted spiritual reality. Inspiration and stimulation flow from the spiritual bodies thus impelling the individual to deliver service and attention to all the kingdoms of nature. The energy of the Cosmic Ray dominating the coordinated personality now gives way to the energy of the Cosmic Ray that is the ruler of the soul extension and thus the individual reaches the state of "soul consciousness" or "group consciousness" which eventually will progress to further expansions of consciousness such as "cosmic consciousness," "God consciousness" and "total oneness consciousness."

This advanced stage implies the development and manifestation of the second Divine Aspect or the energy of Cosmic Ray II of Love/Wisdom which leads to wisdom and illumination under the total rule of intuition and love (Buddhi). Finally, the person must unfold and demonstrate the first Divine Aspect or the energy of Cosmic Ray I of Will/Power/Purpose which means accomplishing a complete synthesis of behavior under the only rule of the dynamic purpose and will of Atma.

DIAGRAM #7
Evolution under the Energies of the Seven Cosmic Rays of Creation

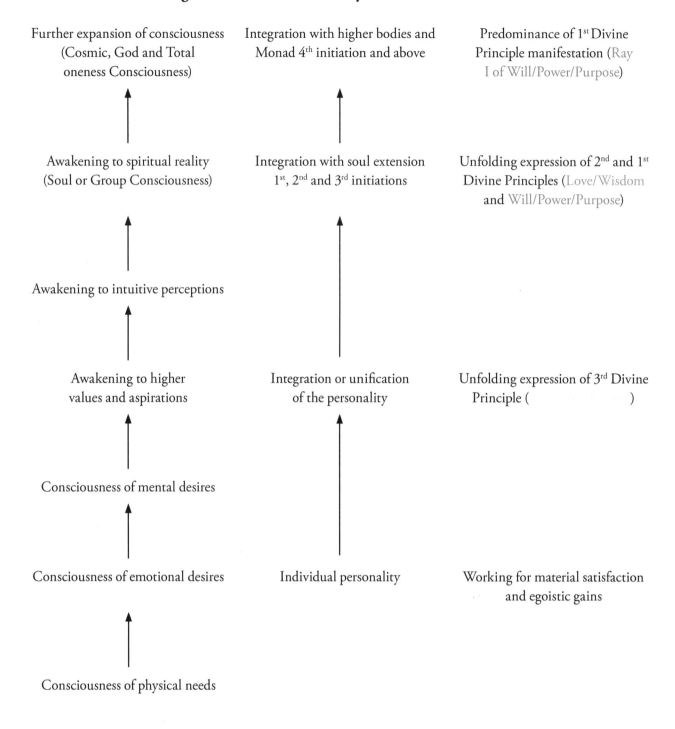

Further expansion of consciousness (Cosmic, God and Total oneness Consciousness)

Integration with higher bodies and Monad 4th initiation and above

Predominance of 1st Divine Principle manifestation (Ray I of Will/Power/Purpose)

Awakening to spiritual reality (Soul or Group Consciousness)

Integration with soul extension 1st, 2nd and 3rd initiations

Unfolding expression of 2nd and 1st Divine Principles (Love/Wisdom and Will/Power/Purpose)

Awakening to intuitive perceptions

Awakening to higher values and aspirations

Integration or unification of the personality

Unfolding expression of 3rd Divine Principle (   )

Consciousness of mental desires

Consciousness of emotional desires

Individual personality

Working for material satisfaction and egoistic gains

Consciousness of physical needs

The energy centers (chakras) open fully.
The electro-magnetic field (aura) becomes
organized into a "Merkabah" shape.

↑

The energy centers (chakras) are in a dormant,
undeveloped state.
The electro-magnetic field (aura) is "egg shaped."

SUMMARY OF OUR PATH AND GOAL THROUGH CONSCIOUS WORK

- Purifying the lower bodies.
- Getting in touch with the soul extension and following its guidance.
- Accomplishing progressive inner understanding.
- Establishing connection with the higher spiritual bodies and allowing them to purify matter totally.
- Exposing the inner light of divinity.
- Ascending to the Fifth Kingdom of Souls.

All this is done by removing layers of darkness and fear in order to reveal the light of pure love and wisdom, as well as to manifest the Will/Power/Purpose of God in our planet.

TABLE #3

4th Kingdom →	Awakening of Consciousness →	5th Kingdom →	Approaching Further Expansions of Consciousness
Focus on the lower bodies (personality). The inner light is hidden. Individuality and separation (ego). Self-consciousness of limitations and mortality.	Many incarnations going through self-discovery and spiritual work. Progressive transformation of the individual, marked by expansions of consciousness (initiations) and increased spiritual awareness. Movement toward a final transmutation and ascension. Integration of higher levels of consciousness.	Focus on the higher bodies (Spirit). Unity and oneness (Group Consciousness). Consciousness of infinity, immortality and divinity.	Approaching Cosmic Consciousness, God or Divine Consciousness and Total Oneness Consciousness.

SUMMARY OF OUR UTMOST OBJECTIVE WHILE INCARNATED IN PLANET EARTH

We come to planetary life in a voyage of exploration and discovery of external realities, as well as internal realities. It is a fantastic chance for learning how to solve problems while existing within an intelligent living form (our lower bodies) which is submerged in a difficult setting of duality. Thus our journey implies pain and suffering but also joy, beauty and hope.

While playing the profound game of life in a physical form, we must learn to find balance in the midst of the opposites that confront us in our day to day existence. We may say that our ultimate objective here is:

- Learn first of all to be a self-standing individual.
- Learn how to deal with emotions.
- Learn how to make the proper choices within this existence of duality and thus develop the lower mind.
- Learn and accept the fact that we are the only ones absolutely responsible for creating the circumstances and conditions of our own lives.
- Learn to experience things without emitting judgments of any kind.
- Find our veritable essence (spirit) and vanish the illusion of our lower self and separation (ego).

This process represents the internal journey that conduces to the center of our being and to higher spiritual realities where peace, mirth, love and union can be experienced. This voyage involves overcoming different obstacles of which ignorance and illusions are the most important, making contact with our spiritual essence and becoming whole again. The beginning of the transformative evolution starts with the recognition of a Supreme Intelligence (God). Then the realization of Its presence within us and in every existing thing, finally accomplishing union with this Superior Force. It is a continuous course that encompasses numerous lifetimes (incarnations) in order to be completed.

We must incorporate in our consciousness the reality of God's love, light and purpose. We must expand the awareness as well as the manifestation of our divinity. This is the time when the apparently physical beings we are start expressing fully the spirituality and oneness that exists within. Now is spirit the sobering, conducting the individual's life in perfect alignment with the Will of God. When we are capable of sustaining a constant state of high degree awareness, we can move beyond restrictions at all levels and allow the divinity within to rule our lives. This is the only truth about our being. We come to learn and internalize the recognition of the divine design within self and the whole creation. We come to reach a state of co-creator.

In this process of growth, we must learn to permit all information coming from the physical senses, feelings and vital force energy to circulate and flow through our being without impediments and blocks. Thus we can really evolve in the direction of our final aim. Also, we must clearly understand that we are not alone in this, we are all together intertwined, including the entire creation, doing the same: growing and evolving. In this manner, each one influences or touches the others in a way in which the achievement of higher degrees of integration by one person has a favorable effect on the advancement of the whole.

- Learn to create our own life in a trustworthy and aware manner, by the right use of the thinking capacity and the right approach to emotions. Also, by allowing love and unity to flow in our relationships.
- Learn to discover our particular mission in each lifetime and carry it on, following the designs of Divine Plan.
- Give to the world the gifts of our soul:
  - Show reverence for all life.
  - Show cooperation and sharing in our actions.
  - Give service and love to all the kingdoms of nature.
  - Aid others to grow spiritually.

SUMMARY OF THE IDEAL MANNER IN WHICH WE SHOULD CONDUCT OUR LIVES

- Honesty.
- Humility.
- Demonstrating our beliefs in our acts.
- Acknowledging spirit and God.
- Developing spiritual practices.
- Doing always the best we can with maximum effort.
- Frequently reviewing our life with willingness to effect changes.
- Dismissing doubts and fears.
- Eliminating controlling attitudes.
- Uprooting anger.
- Vanishing addictions.
- Ending negative criticism, gossip, judgment and complains.
- Living in the now with an accepting attitude.
- Paying attention to the guidance of the soul.
- Being grateful at all times.
- Being a conscious creator of our life and circumstances.
- Loving ourselves and all life.
- Being upholding to others and trying to see the presence of God within them.
- Being alert, open, flexible, spontaneous and free from expectations.

SUMMARY OF THE OUTCOME OF CONSCIOUS SPIRITUAL WORK
At a Mental Level

- Negative thoughts are exchanged by positive ones.
- Doubts are replaced by certainty.
- Thoughts of regret disappear.
- Obsessive thoughts vanish.
- Thinking about past and future lessens.
- The mind appeases and the process of thinking becomes simpler, clearer and direct.
- Problem solving becomes easier.
- The mind turns more lucid.

At an Emotional Level

- Positive feeling of security and protection.
- The feeling of loneliness and isolation disappears.
- Defensiveness disappears.
- Trusting attitude prevails.
- Sensing the presence of God within and around.
- Feeling lighthearted, joyful and peaceful.

At Action Level

- No chaos and struggles.
- Smooth and easy interaction with others.
- Dealing with conflictive situations as observers who are emotionally detached.
- No violence or aggression.
- Achieving things easily.
- Acting calmly with trust.
- Acting with a loving attitude.
- Competition is replaced by cooperation.
- Speaking gently from the heart.

SYNTHESIS

Stages of Awakening Consciousness

- <u>Early Stage</u>: Mainly dedicated to survival and satisfaction of physical needs. The physical body is the center of attention. Stage of ignorance, separation and suffering.
- <u>Middle Stage</u>: Struggle between the inner and outer aspects of the individual. Sense of duality. Beginning of development of the mind through choice-making. Advancing the process of purification and integration of the personality. Beginning of amplification of the
- <u>Advanced Stage</u>: The focus of attention moves toward the soul and spiritual bodies. Moving from "ego consciousness" to "group consciousness." Delivering service to all the kingdoms of nature. Unfolding

of the Second Divine Aspect of Love/Wisdom **and finally also of the** First Divine Aspect of Will/ Purpose/Power.

Our Spiritual Path and Goal

- Purification of the lower bodies (physical – emotional – mental).
- Contact with the soul extension.
- Progressive inner understanding.
- Contact with the higher spiritual bodies.
- Exposure of the inner light.
- Ascension to the Fifth Kingdom.

Our Main Purpose while Incarnated

- Learn individuality.
- Learn to deal with emotions.
- Learn to make right choices through experiencing duality.
- Take responsibility as the creators of the circumstances of our own lives.
- Learn to experience without judgment.
- Discover our true nature (spirit) and vanish separation (ego).
- Learn to be conscious co-creators of our lives.
- Discover our especial mission in each life and see its connection to the Divine Plan.
- Offer the gifts of our soul to the world and help others on the path.

How to Ideally Conduct our Life

- Honesty and humility.
- Consistency between talk and act.
- Maximum effort to do the best possible.
- Accepting personal fails and willingness to change.
- Work to eliminate doubts, fears, anger, addictions, negative criticism, complains, gossip and judgment.
- Being loving and grateful.
- Acknowledging spirit and God.
- Developing spiritual practices.
- Following guidance from the soul.
- Living in the present and accepting it as it is at the moment.
- Being alert, open, flexible and spontaneous.
- Seeing the presence of God in everything and everybody.

Outcome of Spiritual Work

Mental level:
- A lucid and calm mind, with positive thoughts and concentrated only in the present moment.
- Clear, simple and direct thinking.
- Easy problem-solving.

Emotional level:

- Trusting attitude with no defensiveness.
- Feeling peaceful, joyful and protected.
- Sensing God within and without.

Action level:

- Calm action with a loving and trusting attitude.
- Speaking directly from the heart.
- Smooth interaction with others.
- Non-violence, no struggles and achieving with ease.
- Conflicts are solved from an emotionally detached point of view.
- Cooperation prevails.

CHAPTER VIII

PRAYER AND MEDITATION

<u>Prayer</u>

Prayer has the purpose of attaining contact with a higher spiritual being, or with our own superior being and God. Thus, through it, the human being consciously seeks attunement with spiritual forces. Prayer, as a verbal outpouring movement of the individual personality, is ultimately a call to God and a conversation with God. Consequently, the pure aim of prayer is to experience our own relationship of oneness with God.

True prayer should not be directed to asking for escape, absolution or an easy alleviation. Instead it should ask for help with the necessary strength and clarity of mind to go through a given situation that has been already accepted by us as part of our learning experience, or to find remedy to a problem, or to request aid for others.

Prayer is in reality a forceful instrument that can be used in the process of human transformation and spiritual growth. As we advance on the spiritual path, the quotient of light increases in our being, thus prayer in the form of a request for more light, which is pure intelligence, brings toward us light beings from the spiritual realms that surely will assist; allowing us to gain clarity and power to solve our conflicts.

The traits of authentic prayer are:

- Faith and trust in a higher force (God).
- Attitude of surrendering to the will of the higher force and recognition that the will of God is ultimately our own will that has only remained hidden from our awareness.
- Honestly, meaningfully and intelligently formulated.
- Deeply heartfelt.
- Manifestation of profound love for self, others and God.
- Manifestation of deep gratitude.
- Manifestation of unselfishness, by including others.

Prayers may have different formats as follows:

- Solicitation or petition.
- Disclosure or confession.
- Gratitude and thanksgiving.
- Veneration or glorification of God.
- Affirmation of total submission to God's will, which is the highest form of prayer.

Meditation

Meditation implies elevating our awareness toward realms of a higher vibratory frequency where we establish contact with our soul extension and spiritual bodies. Hence, we can experience the spiritual worlds where we exist as such. Thus, meditation is the means by which we can move beyond the limitations of the intellectual mind and enter a state of super-consciousness where the continuous internal dialogue of the lower mind is discontinued. In the silence of meditation, we communicate with our higher self and God, listening then to the "divine language."

In general, our attention is dispersed throughout the body and extends outwardly by means of the sensory perceptions. The act of meditation starts with the abstraction or withdrawal of the physical senses from the external objective world of things, including our physical body, then shifting the focus of attention within and concentrating it at a single point. This single point could be something external and tangible such as an image, a flower, an element of water, or a flame. Or it could be entirely internal such as the area of the Third Eye Chakra or the Heart Chakra. Thus we concentrate our mind and feeling on that point which serves the purpose of allowing contact with the soul and the flowing stream of sound and light capable of transporting us beyond our physical consciousness toward higher states of consciousness and the source of creation. At this point, meditation is relaxing and resting within oneself, as well as expanding toward unrestricted existence.

In order to help the focusing of the mind in one point, it is recommended to pay attention to and follow the phases of the breath, since the act of breathing has a direct connection with the human mind as well as the natural motion of creation that involves expansion/contraction (the "breath of God"). By means of focusing on the process of breathing, the mind can become calmer and we can attune to the entire creation. Also it will help to focus the mind and move toward inner consciousness when we fix our gaze in one point, not allowing our eyes to move from object to object, since the eye movements are also directly connected to the mind. In addition, following the phases of respiration may be coupled with silently repeating the "breath mantra" SO – HUM: SO, while inhaling, and HUM while exhaling.

Meditation is to enter within a quiet space of absolute silence, without any kind of expectation. We must not practice it thinking that we are going to be elevated, enlightened, or have fantastic visions. The complete immobility and silence of the lower mind generates extraordinary energy represented by the creative forces pouring in from above, bringing knowledge and wisdom. The latest were blocked and impeded by the ceaseless activity of the intellect that permanently keeps us paying attention only to the external world.

The nature of the lower mind is per se ceaseless activity, producing an interminable chain of thoughts. And this is exactly what happens naturally when we sit on meditation; however, in the same natural way (without forcing it), the mind can reach a state of stillness and its turbulence can be appeased. This takes place when we learn to act as witness of our own mental activity. We step back and only observe the thoughts parading one after another, without engaging with them. That is not judging, not developing, not following them; just letting their motion be without any resistance. Then two things may happen: First, we suddenly realize that the one observing is not the "I" we usually identify with (the physical body, nor emotional body, neither the lower mental body) but another entity (the soul); and secondly, amazingly there is no more thoughts, only universal silence and the mind is finally quiet. Within this silence, a new and different movement begins which is the pure action of the soul that does not belong in time nor needs verbal expression. The mind becomes motionless and clear, cleansed from all former conditioning. And this is the only state of mind in which truth can be seen, for a mind that acts mechanically and is frantically busy can never approach the truth of Supreme Order. Only when we are transformed into an empty vessel can the divine forces descend to fill us up.

Through the practice of meditation, we learn mastery of the lower mind. We use the mind only when we need it in our daily life and also we can silence it at will and thus be free from its endless noise. In this way, meditation brings us to a state of complete freedom from all we have learned and known, as well as a state where the mind becomes pure, empty space.

In a true meditative state the physical, emotional and lower mental bodies are aligned in consonance with the spiritual fountain of cosmic order and the mind turns still and silent, but also acutely attentive. This would allow for a clear, impersonal observation of the totality of consciousness, without any element of distortion; all our attention now is focused on internally listening and seeing. In this state, new parts of the brain that have nothing to do with thought processes become functional and ready instruments for the activity of soul/spirit. Meditation then implicates the awakening of the soul's energy and going beyond the tumultuous lower or intellectual mind that represents "ego consciousness." Thus to contact the soul, the intellectual mind must be bypassed. In this manner the soul is liberated and permitted to act within its own spiritual realm. Now it really begins the activity of true intelligence, compassion and love.

Meditation may be considered as an inner pilgrimage that conduces to encounter with the true Self, through looking profoundly within and becoming more and more aware of spiritual reality. Meditation thus puts us in a pure state of attention which is completely de-voided of what is called "I consciousness," as it is full with a loving feeling and awareness of the total unity of life. Hence, meditation is a movement away from fragmentation and separation toward wholeness. It is the end of linear time. It moves closer to the heart and love as it moves away from the logic of the lower mind.

Regarding the subject of meditation, the different modalities and techniques utilized are not really important. What really matters is an honest, profound and intense desire to re-connect with the Self and the Supreme Being. When we practice in this manner, a vortex of energy is created that acts as a conduit for communication with higher realms and through which spiritual energy can penetrate the earth.

Going further, meditation is not only to sit in quiet and silence but a process, a whole movement, a state of mind that we should continue and extend to every minute of our daily living, not limiting it only to the moments of traditional practice. Thus our everyday activities can also become a form of meditation if we act from a center of silence within and if we keep the mind clear and full of space. In order to do that, we must learn to totally resolve each problem or challenge in our lives immediately as they appear; we must not carry any burden, and that will create space within the mind.

Effects Resulting from the Practice of Meditation

- Improves the general physical health by means of relaxation which diminishes the levels of stress.
- Augments the energy flow throughout the physical body, revitalizing and strengthening it by the stimulation of the energy centers or chakras. It recharges us and removes existing blocks of energy.
- Slows down the process of aging by changing the frequency of wave patterns and chemistry in the brain.
- Quiets the mind and this in turn contributes to physical relaxation.
- Reduces chronic pain by loosening the awareness that is focused on the physical body.
- Helps to improve health problems such as hypertension, insomnia, asthma, and heart, stomach and intestinal disturbances.
- Improves the mental/emotional health by inducing a relaxed state and helping us to handle emotions and thoughts in a calmer and detached manner.
- Increases our chance to truly experience joy and love since we are exposed to contact with higher spiritual forces.

- Increases sensitivity to everything and develops the intuitive quality.
- Helps to diminish fears, anxiety, anger, lack of self-appreciation and violent expressions.
- Helps to develop patience, tolerance, compassion, understanding, caring and love.
- Meditation is the principal medium by which we grow spiritually and progress to concretely express our inner divine qualities. Our spiritual advancement is marked by the following:
  - We gain awareness of our soul and divine powers and thus discover our inner beauty, peace and love.
  - We purify through exposure to cosmic light forces.
  - We escape from egotistic ego influences and the prison of the intellectual mind.
  - We contact our own inner Spirit/Divinity and become increasingly more conscious of it.
  - We discover an endless source of truth/wisdom and learn to go deep inside with our questions.
  - We acquire experiential knowledge of the inner spiritual worlds.
  - We realize the temporal and transitory character of the outer physical world and thus ordinary problems in life do not affect us anymore in the same way.
  - We lose the fear of death.
  - We realize that others are soul/spirit as much as we are and all belong to one family existing in unity within the God Force.
  - We respect and help others and the environment in which we live.
  - We realize the tremendous importance of everything existing around us.
  - Our way of life becomes "non-violence" per se: no ill-thinking, no harsh speech, no hurting anybody nor anything. Life turns richer and intense, by the presence of joy and love.
- Opens a door, so allowing the inner reality to guide the outer life.
- Betters our external conditions by:
  - Augmenting our ability of focusing attention and concentration which increases our efficiency in worldly tasks.
  - Increasing our capacity to listen more and react less to others.
  - Improving our aptitude for problem solving, since keeping our connection with higher spiritual existence supports our mind with peace and clarity.
  - Helping our dexterity to make good choices, when learning through meditation to look at things from a higher perspective.
  - Better achieving a state of inner peace, we radiate it and influence positively the external world around us.
  - Our life becomes wholly meaningful and transforms into a sacred way of existence. This is possible by achieving a state of mind that translates in maintaining constant alertness and attentiveness from a central point of peace and silence.

DIAGRAM #8

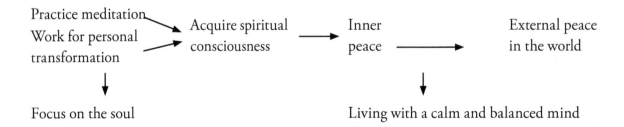

and develop: Humility – Honesty – Non-violence – Purity – Universal love

In summary, meditation involves:

- Withdrawal from the external world and shift of attention to the inner world.
- Relaxation and calmness of the physical body.
- Concentration and focusing the mind by following the phases of respiration slowly and repeating silently the "breath mantra": SO-HUM. By quieting the breathing the mind becomes calmer.
- Appeasing the mind. The aim of meditation is to cease for a while the process of thinking and have the opportunity to look at the spirit within. All thoughts must be released in a passive and quiet manner. We ought to observe the coming thoughts but making no effort to stop them, as well as remaining detached from them. We allow them without engaging with them, until they naturally disappear.
- Contacting the soul energy.
- Reaching a state of contemplation which is nothing but the soul in action.

Meditation brings about:

- Refreshment of the mind.
- Order in the mind.
- Meaning and purpose to living.
- Inner self-confidence and freedom.
- Transformation of ourselves and our circumstances.
- Transcendence of the limitations of the lower mind (intellect).
- Increased receptivity to divine light and spirit (the Cosmic Mind).

TABLE #4

PRAYER	MEDITATION
We feel separated from God.	We feel God deeply within us.
We invoke and talk to God.	We listen to God.
We petition and wait for grace to come to us.	We do not ask for anything, we just melt into and commune with God.
Purifies the mind and heart.	Illumines the mind and heart.
Augments the receptivity to God Force.	We enter the infinite and melt in it.
We call and feel moving upward: rising	We feel infinitely growing and enlarging: dissolving.
Frequently prayer is for our own selves and our dear ones.	Meditation is all-inclusive. We feel oneness.

Eventually, when the practice of meditation is advanced, prayer is no longer needed. We discover and realize that the God Force knows everything about us and we surrender our limited will to Divine Will.

SYNTHESIS

- Prayer establishes contact with higher spiritual forces and God.
- Prayer is a call to God and a conversation with God.
- True prayer asks for strength to go through a given situation in life and clarity of mind for self and others.
- Prayer can be an instrument for spiritual growth since it brings more light to our being.
- The characteristics of authentic prayer are:
  - Faith and trust.
  - Surrendering.
  - Honesty and deep feeling.
  - Love for self, others and God.
  - Unselfishness and gratitude.
- Meditation should be practiced without any expectations.
- Meditation implies rising our awareness to higher spiritual worlds and making contact with our soul, Monad and God.
- Meditation is going beyond the limitations of the intellectual mind (ego) and entering a state of super-consciousness and union with God (everything existing).
- Meditation is silence and listening to God.
- Meditation begins with withdrawal of attention from the external world and focus on the inner world.
- It continues with relaxation and following the phases of breathing as well as simultaneous concentration on a single point (external or internal).
- Next is the quieting of the mind by accepting and observing all the arising thoughts without trying to stop them but remaining detached, only witnessing until they simply vanish without any effort on our part.
- Then, contact with the soul ensues, followed by contemplation of the activity of the soul and higher realms (melting into God Force).
- Meditation is an inner journey to encounter the true Self. It is a pure state of attention and absolute union with all life.
- Meditation is a movement toward heart and love and away from the separation of the lower mind.
- The meditative state can be extended to daily activities, for our benefit.
- The persistent practice of meditation conduces to:
  - Improvement of general health (physical, emotional and mental) through relaxation.
  - Increased energy and re-vitalization.
  - Mastery of the lower mind (learning how to silence it and when to use it).
  - Increased opportunities to experience joy and love.
  - Increased sensitivity.
  - Development of the intuitive capacity.
  - Development of patience, tolerance and compassion.
  - Spiritual growth and purification.
  - Contact with our soul/spirit.
  - Discovery of truth.

- Expansion of wisdom.
- Experiential knowledge of the inner spiritual worlds.
- Wiser approach to the problems inherent in daily life or life on the planet.
- Loss of the fear of death.
- Realization of the unity of everything.
- More respect for others, the environment and the other kingdoms of nature.
- Non-violence at all levels (physical/mental).
- Trusting spirit as our guide.
- Improvement of the external conditions in living.

CHAPTER IX

TYPES AND PRACTICE OF MEDITATION

Recommended Exercises (to be practiced before engaging in a consistent practice of meditation)

1 Observing

Train yourself and learn to be a conscious observer. Start by watching your physical body in activity: while walking, talking, eating, sitting, bathing, etc; really watching it. Later, progress to watching your emotional and mental bodies: be totally aware of your feelings, reactions, moods and thoughts. Let go the mechanical, automatic mode of living. Become fully aware, conscious and present at each moment of your life.

The observer we are referring to is in reality the soul of the person. By practicing in this manner, we learn to live absolutely in the now and in touch with our soul extension.

2 Embracing

Closing the eyes, while sitting, embrace each and everything about you at that moment: your body, your breathing, your thinking, your feelings and sensations. Be conscious of the unity of all that. Then allow yourself to gradually expand outward until you can embrace and include within yourself the entirety of the cosmos.

3 Using the physical senses as doors of access to spiritual realities

Smelling

Deeply smell a perfume, a flower or incense. Then walk away slowly. The scent now becomes gradually less and your awareness of it sharpens in order to perceive it. Continue moving away until the aroma vanishes and you realize it is missing and there is nothingness in its place. This is the moment when we can connect with something higher.

Looking

Stare at something. Then look at the absence of the object. Look at nothingness and enter a higher state of mind.

Listening
- Listen attentively to a melody. Then stop it and listen to the silence of its absence.
- With closed eyes listen to each and every sound occurring within and around you. The sounds of creation are coming to you as if you were the center that attracts and absorbs them all. Absolute silence and peace ensues and your consciousness flies higher and higher.

4 <u>Discarding</u>

Cast away your entire present luggage. Let go of your tension, rigidity, restlessness, emotional disturbance and thoughts. Enter into relaxation, trust and peace. This practice maybe aided by doing in unison any kind of physical movement (exercise or dance); also by laughter.

5 <u>Watching the breath</u>

We must learn to follow all the natural phases of respiration:

- Inhalation that represents being born to physical life.
- Pause, while life is being distributed all over our being.
- Exhalation that symbolizes letting go and dying.
- Pause, while merging in the "eternal now" happens.
- With closed eyes, begin to gently follow your breath as the air goes in and out. Allow yourself to be totally aware only of the respiration process and move with it in a continuous flow. Thus consciousness and breath become one. Then, move your attention to the short and subtle pauses between inhalations and exhalations, and vice versa. This is the cero point where no movement exists, this is the eternal now. Try to keep focused only in the gap, in the pause as your breathing continues naturally.

<u>The Actual Practice of Meditation</u>

In the practice of meditation we should not follow rigid rules, in spite of what we generally hear about it. The following are general guidelines: The posture could be as simple as sitting on a chair in a comfortable, relaxed manner with feet flat on the ground, closed or open eyes and hands resting on the lap with palms open upward. The back should be kept straight, facilitating the flow of energy through the central energy centers or chakras along the spinal cord.

If the eyes are open it is best to cast the gaze front and downward, allowing it to expand and diffuse. This is known as "relaxing the gaze," since this facilitates the access to a meditative state of mind;or, to look at something such as a flower, a crystal, a flame, which will aid in invoking certain states of inspiration and peace. Also the gaze can be directed to observe the image of a spiritual master which will help in connecting with the spiritual truth embodied therein that is resonating with our own inner nature.

The hands, as another alternative, can be placed covering the knees, or together where the left palm upward contains the right hand that is equally keeping the palm upward with the tip of the thumbs gently touching each other. We can also have the option to sit in a lotus or half lotus position.

The breath, at the beginning, can be used as a means to release tension in general (physical, emotional and mental), letting it go with each exhalation. We ought to breathe slowly, deeply, rhythmically and abdominally, if possible. The best attitude to maintain is that of not expecting any pre-conceived ideas to manifest, not setting any kind of goal to achieve, and not looking for any results. Very early morning hours are the most propitious for this practice.

Finally, it would be ideal if posterior to a practice of meditation, we could remain in a centered and calm state of mind which then can be transferred to each and all activities of our daily life, allowing us to be entirely present at all moments.

The wake state in a human being is characterized by presenting brain waves which are called beta waves that possess a high frequency of above 13.5 Hz/second. The relaxed and receptive state of meditation produces the appearance of alpha waves in the brain activity, which exhibit a frequency between 7.5 and 13.4 Hz/second. During a deep meditative state, the brain waves become theta waves with frequencies between 3.5 and 7.4 Hz/second. The later research conducted on meditation subjects shows that certain persons who are capable of producing pure states of love and compassion in themselves while meditating, manifest changes in the activity of their brains that demonstrate a diffuse activation of different systems in specific parts of the brain, which produce a synchronic and integrated pattern of so called gamma waves band oscillations.

Different Types of Meditation

1 – Guided Meditation

This type of meditation can be either self-guided or lead by another person. It consists of:

- Sitting comfortably with closed eyes.
- Relaxing the physical body.
- Using creative imagination to bring beams of light to the chakras or to the body in general, with the purpose of cleansing, activating and vitalizing.
- Following certain commands of action for encouragement and correction.
- Visualizing images, actions or stories.
- Silently and mentally repeating positive affirmations to reinforce attitudes and to program the subconscious part of the mind with beneficial seeds.

The use of imagination must be accompanied by corresponding feelings. Developing the capacity for creative imagination brings about the opening up of new brain pathways, as well as it stimulates the pineal gland to absorb high energy in the form of light.

A good practice to use creative imagination is trying to see our own body internally. With closed eyes and sitting in a relaxed posture we move our focus of attention to the Third Eye chakra and then initiate an internal voyage throughout our body (from toes to head), bringing our consciousness to each part and seeing it. This exercise helps in bringing us to the realization that the real self is not the physical body. At that moment, we notice that the observer of the physical body is something else, beyond it; thus we can easily move away from identification with the physical body. And further, by observing our mind, we can do the same; break free from it.

Another example of the use of creative imagination is the following:

- Sit comfortably relaxed with closed eyes.
- Imagine a gentle shower of pure, bright, white light falling on you as a refreshing rain.
- See and feel you being cleansed and purified. Let go voluntarily all impurities from your body.
- See and feel your body absorbing this light and becoming pure light itself.
- See yourself standing within a column of white light that connects the heights with the center of Earth.
- See yourself irradiating this light from your body in all directions.

2 – <u>Deep Meditation or Witnessing Meditation</u>

Practicing this kind of meditation we penetrate through the clamor of the lower mind, ego consciousness and physical body identification to reach a state that is beyond the grasp of the physical world. This meditation progresses through the following steps:

- Relaxation
- Concentration
- Meditation
- Contemplation
- Inspiration

<u>Relaxation</u>

- Sit on a chair or on the floor in a relaxed posture as described formerly; eyes open or closed.
- Breathe slowly and deeply.
- Become totally aware of your physical body at first. How it feels and how it does. Watch it, paying full attention. This attitude opens the door to relaxation and peace.
- Intentionally relax each part of the body, from feet upward to head. Use the aid of following the breath in order to release all tension with each exhalation.
- Calmly shift your awareness to the subtler level of your thoughts and just watch. This too helps to open the door to relaxation and peace, and creates a bridge between body and mind.

<u>Concentration</u>

As a usual situation, our attention is most of the time wandering through different outer pleasures and attractions of the external world. Our focus is constantly moving here and there, following the experiences of our physical senses and emotions. It is disseminated throughout our body and lower mind, with which we mainly identify, living thus unaware of our true nature.

Concentration implies giving absolute and total attention to one specific thing. In this state there is no separation, no duality; only full attention with no movement of the mind. This puts us in a state of inner alertness and vigilance, facilitating the elevation of consciousness toward higher levels by the withdrawal of attention from the external world and the shift to the inner world. The focus of our attention may be placed on any of the following:

- <u>The breath</u>

This is called "conscious breathing" and implies watching our breathing carefully, in its four phases, and following it naturally and effortlessly (inhalation – pause – exhalation – pause). Each time your focus moves away from the breathing process being distracted either by an external noise or a thought or a physical sensation, bring it back to the breath, disregarding how many times is necessary to do it. This practice aids in calming and training the mind.

So, observe the breath first, then become one with it and eventually even the focus on the breath will dissolve, as it does the ego identity.

- <u>The Third Eye chakra</u>

In this case, we close our eyes and bring our entire consciousness to focus internally only on the area of the Third Eye chakra. We thus retire from the external world and center ourselves inwardly. By closing and focusing the eyes inward, we help ourselves to come out of the sense of duality.

- <u>The Heart chakra</u>

If we choose this, we should bring our full attention and feeling to the heart area and remain there, feeling a sensation of warmth. This is the place of our inner altar.

- <u>A word or a mantra</u>

This should be repeated either silently or loudly, slowly and heartedly, with feelings. We must deeply feel the core or essence of the word, thus its vibrations take over the entire being and help to bring about a positive feeling or even invoke the profound true essence of our soul. Examples of words that can be used for this purpose are: Any of the used names for God, love, light, peace, or joy. Examples of mantras could be:" OM/ AUM" (the sound of creation) or "SO HUM" (the silent mantra of the breath).

- <u>A sound</u>

We may choose to concentrate our attention in listening only to a sound that could be external or internal, such as the sound of the heart beat or the sound of the breath.

The next following modalities involve observing or looking with very intense alertness; in this manner, being deeply present, the mind instantly ceases its motion. So, if we choose to focus our attention on something while keeping the eyes open, it could be:

- <u>A flower</u>

In this case we are becoming one with the color, perfume, beauty, harmony and giving capacity of the flower.

- <u>A candle</u>

We become one with the flame which is a symbol of illumination and clarity. The essence of it can thus penetrate the mind and burn all thoughts.

- <u>The image of a spiritual master, or a symbol, or a mandala</u>

For instance, the symbol to be used could be the one that represents the mantra "OM": ॐ

When we choose to practice concentration with open eyes, after a while, we must close the eyes and see the image that we were looking at internally (with our imagination), at the area of the Third Eye chakra. If our mind gets disrupted with thoughts we must bring it back to the image held at the Third Eye chakra, again and again, as in the case of following the breath. This will render the mind engaged in one focus instead of being wandering around.

The step of concentration may be achieved also by combining some of the above examples. For instance, focusing on the breath in unison with focusing on one or both of the mentioned chakras (Third Eye or Heart), by looking internally behind the eyes and feeling in the heart area. Also, to the former can be added focusing on the silent mantra of the breath (SO-HUM).

So the main purpose of the step of concentration is to quiet and focus the mind. A peaceful mind will happen when the process of thinking wears away and disappears. We must observe the parade of thoughts arising within our mind and allow them to happen, without fighting them or engaging with them, without resistance to their content, justification or judgment; in other words, not feeding them. We just look at them as a separate, silent witness. Finally they shall evaporate, bringing the mind to stillness. So we observe our thought patterns, we witness, in a resting, detached, objective state. This will eventually conduce us to the transcendence of thought.

In alike fashion we must observe not only our thoughts but also our feelings, sensations and impulses; allow them to flow and then let them go; thus we become free, with a mind that is no longer disturbed by the past or the future.

Meditation

At this stage, we approach the creative splendor of the current of sound and light that inundates and conduces us to a higher state of expanded consciousness and serenity. Visions of images and lights can be experienced within this state. Lights of different colors are reflections from higher realms and images may be those from the astral world or belonging to our personal subconscious level or to the collective subconscious level. It is like a voyage retracing the contents of the deeper layers of our mind.

Contemplation

Now we contact our soul/spirit and enter a state of pure contemplation, resting within the "eternal now." We are totally aware of our true being and God. Although a sense of self is still present, there appears an expanded sense of unity with the entire cosmos, which represents the states of cosmic and divine consciousness. This is being absolutely and totally awaken, a condition characterized by complete merging and sharing. We become acutely conscious of being part of infinity, eternity and that force we call God. Everything becomes one indivisible flow of consciousness and everything is held within us. The mind becomes emptiness, silence and peace. There are no thoughts, no forms, no fear; but bliss and power. We reach the state of pure consciousness and light, without content; which is the veritable essence of the Self, beyond form and name. This condition of joy, peace and pure being is immovable and is not contingent to what we do or possess in life.

Inspiration

This stage consists in extending the results and the learning from the meditation practice to the confines of daily living as concrete expression and application. The former implies to remain in a steady state of calm and happiness while living in the physical realm; we radiate it outwardly. As a consequence of this condition, we transform our attitude and reactions toward others and life circumstances. Our actions then originate from a center of understanding and compassion, with total awareness of the oneness of everything.

Achieving steady higher states of consciousness produce a natural movement of the inner power outward, and this can be utilized to assist and help others in need. Thus, the light and purity of the soul/spirit is poured out from our hearts and minds and our daily life becomes literally a meditation in itself.

Some of the sensations that might be experienced while practicing this type of meditation are:

- Sensation of heat in the hands and/or the head.
- Sensation of tingling in the extremities and/or along the spine.
- Sensation of heat and expansion of the chakras.
- Sensation of spinning or experiencing involuntary body movements, such as moving the upper part of the body back and forth, or side to side.
- Sensation of expansion of the whole body.
- Sense of being out of the body.
- Sensation of electrical currents running through the body.

3 – <u>Walking Meditation</u>

This kind of meditation can be practiced in any location or specifically walking a labyrinth. The concentration and focus is placed on the breath and on each step that is taken. Breath and steps can be synchronized. The breathing should be slow and rhythmic. The steps should also be slow and the person must remain fully aware of them, feeling each movement of the legs and feet, as well as their contact with the earth. The hands can be kept in a position such as making a fist with the right hand which is contained within the palm of the left hand; and resting thus both hands over the solar plexus area. The eyes are kept looking downward.

Labyrinths are of special significance since they represent the different paths we walk and wander through in third dimensional life; they symbolize the bridge, between this dimension and higher ones, that allows our exit. We walk the labyrinth through a path that conduces to the central point; and this point depicts the access to the upright axis linking all dimensions of existence. Labyrinths are part of what we call terrestrial sacred geometry; that is, focal vortex points where connection with other dimensions is made possible due to the generated arrangements of energy. In treading a labyrinth we touch our multidimensional makeup and along the required turning movements, to the right and to the left, our sense of duality wears away while our entire being is inundated with a new sensation of oneness and unity.

Further, following the labyrinth's path causes the vital energy in our body to vigorously circulate through the energy centers or chakras, which induce us to move along the various states of consciousness represented by each chakra. This act has a powerful cleansing, refreshing and revitalizing repercussion on our bodies and minds.

4 - <u>Nature Meditation</u>

This type of meditation entails a prolonged contemplation of some chosen element of nature such as:

- The sky (day or night).
- Fire.
- A body of water.
- A mountain.
- A rock.
- A tree, plant or flower.
- The moon.

Practicing in this way we achieve a total identification with the object of contemplation up to the point where there is no longer any difference or separation between us and the object, thus time disappears. We melt into the object; we empty ourselves of everything and lose individuality. We become peaceful and relaxed.

Another manner of practicing nature meditation is the following:

With closed eyes, be acutely alert and listen to each of the different sounds in nature that are happening around you at the moment. With absolute acceptance embrace each and everything around you. Merely listen outwardly and watch yourself inwardly. Remain totally relaxed and calm, without any conflict or resistance.

5 - Activity or Life Meditation

Practicing this type of meditation we must put our entire attention and concentrate solely in the activity, whatever it might be that we are performing at each given moment of our daily life. We must immerse ourselves totally and feel it profoundly until we become it and nothing else exists for us. We become absolutely that which we are doing, with total awareness and presence. We are very alert and cognizant of everything involved in the particular task: our movements, thoughts, feelings, etc. We no longer perform in an automatic manner.

Another way of practicing life meditation is when we live consciously recognizing the presence of Divinity all around us and we dedicate all our activities and work to God. If we are capable of feeling God's presence in whatever activity we do, we are always with the God force and we live a life of compassion, love and expansion. This is a sacred way of living. Our mind suffers a transformation that allows us to live in a permanent state of meditation.

Recommended Exercise to Practice after Meditation

1 – Becoming more alert and awake

Stop for a moment and observe an object (plant, flower, etc) with intent and alertness; slowly observe each detail: color, form, vibrancy….

SYNTHESIS

Exercises Prior to Meditation

- Observing (everything).
- Embracing (your parts and everything else).
- Using the physical senses as doors of access to higher states of consciousness.
- Discarding (your luggage and burdens).
- Watching the breath (inhalation – pause – exhalation – pause).

Practice of Meditation

- Neither rigid rules nor expectations nor specific goals.
- Relaxed posture sitting in a chair or lotus position on the floor.
- Straight spine and feet on the floor.
- Closed or open eyes.

- Hands resting on the lap with open palms upward, or covering the knees with palms downward, or together in a mudra position.
- Breathing used to release tension first, and to concentrate later (slow, deep and rhythmic).
- Posterior to the practice, transfer the centered and calm state of mind to daily activities.

Different Types of Meditation

1 – Guided Meditation (self-guided or guided by someone else)

Involves the use of creative imagination and visualization with light, imaginary actions, or silently repeating positive affirmations.

Examples:
- Watching our body internally.
- Shower of white light.

2 – Deep or Witnessing Meditation

Steps:
- Relaxation: using the breath.
- Concentration: using the breath, Third Eye chakra, Heart chakra, a word or a mantra, sound, a flower, a candle, or the image of a spiritual master.
- Meditation: trip that retraces the different layers of the mind.
- Contemplation: contact with soul/spirit. Experience of oneness, infinity and pure joy.
- Inspiration: extension of the meditative learning to daily living through concrete application of it.

3 – Walking Meditation

- Practiced in any place, or walking a labyrinth.
- Focus on breath and each step (walk and breathe slowly).
- Labyrinths are terrestrial sacred geometry or places that facilitate connection with other higher dimensions.

4 – Nature Meditation

- Sustained contemplation of an element of nature, or listening, with closed eyes, to all surrounding sounds.
- Achieving total union with the objects of contemplation and embracing all.

5 – Activity or Life Meditation

- Becoming totally present in each daily activity and moving out of automatic actions.
- Recognizing the presence of God in everything, being and activity.
- Dedicating our acts and work to God (living sacredly).

Exercise Posterior to Meditation

- Becoming more alert by slowing down and observing things externally as well as internally.

CHAPTER X

AIDS TO MEDITATION

<u>Yantras</u>

The words "yantra" and "mandala" are commonly used in an interchangeable manner. However, there is a very subtle difference between them. The word yantra means "instrument;" also "to hold." Yantras are constructed by drawing geometric forms which are combined in different patterns that represent the energy of thought forms or divine ideas. Then, yantras are symbolic instruments that hold and sustain thought forms which conduct energy through the various dimensions of existence, since in a yantra are contained those thought forms that represent the multiple levels or dimensions of existence. They depict the manifested aspect, as well as the unmanifested side of Divinity.

A yantra may be produced by using not only geometrical forms but also adding floral patterns and universal symbols. The geometrical figures used with this purpose are considered part of what we call sacred geometry (shapes found throughout creation that consists of energy patterns with a given meaning). These most commonly are: The circle, the triangle and the square.

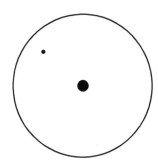

The shape of a circle encompasses the highest energy. It represents:

The Creator

The eternal.

The infinite (no beginning and no end)

Spirit

The cosmos

Oneness

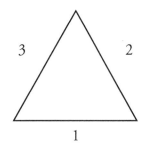

The shape of a triangle is as well a very powerful energy, related to the beginning of creation and manifestation. It represents the Holy Trinity or the three divine aspects of God, which are present all through creation:

Will/Purpose/Power

Love/Wisdom

Active Intelligence

In a human being, we may correlate these aspects with Body/Mind/Spirit or Personality/Higher Self/Monad.

The shape of the square implies the presence of a symbolic cross at the center. It Represents:

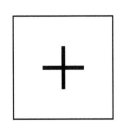

Physical manifestation
Being born
The four cardinal points (direction)
The four basic chemical elements (N – H – C – O)
The four nature elements (Earth – Water – Fire – Air)
Structure
Heaven (the vertical line of the cross), Earth (the horizontal line of the cross) and their meeting point (the central point)

Balance

Also, yantras may be regarded as a diagram expression of a mantra, both representing aspects of Divinity. The most widely known form of yantra is the one called "Sri Yantra" which means "Gate to the Heavens." It is usually created from the center (Creator) outwards and represents the beginning of creation (triangles), the different levels of evolutionary paths (concentric circles enclosed within a bigger circle, and physical manifestation, symbolized by the outer square with four gates at the middle point of its sides, which represent the four cardinal points of direction. The Sri Yantra may as well be considered as a visual mantra that transmits the sound of "OM" or "AUM" (sound of creation).

Mandalas

The word "mandala" means "circle." A mandala is a type of yantra composed by concentric geometrical figures which are drawn around a central point that symbolizes the Source or Divinity and from which everything spirals out. Thus a mandala is a sacred pattern or geometrical depiction of the entire cosmos and God the Creator.

Mandalas are symbolic images or reflections of the cosmos, as well as of the human soul that may be considered as the point of access to the subtler levels of existence. Therefore, we may view mandalas as a symbolic language that guides through doorways into the soul, the cosmos and the Creator; also as a sacred space portraying the different states of consciousness. Mandalas embody the characteristics of symmetry and balance.

Both yantras and mandalas can be utilized for the following:

- To establish or complete a sacred space in our home or place of learning.
- As instruments for spiritual teachings.
- As a focus of attention to develop concentration capacity.
- To develop the faculties of observation and re-creative internal visualization.
- To stimulate a state of mental quietness.
- To bring about a state of equilibrium, integration and wholeness.
- As a chart to follow the paths conducive to the center of being.
- To connect with our soul and everything in creation.

- To understand more profoundly the symbols, patterns and energy currents in creation, their interconnectedness and their relation to our own being.
- As a conveyer of healing.
- As a meditation aid.

When used in the practice of meditation, yantras and mandalas are visual metaphors of the underlying essence of creation and the cosmos that become instruments for focusing attention (concentration), evoking higher states of consciousness, and guiding us on the path to reunion with Divinity through intuitive knowing by tapping into the language of the soul. The meditating person mentally penetrates the mandala and travels through the different states of consciousness that lead to the center of all. By looking attentively to yantras or mandalas, we are literally directing our mind energy toward God.

So, to finalize, yantras are pictorial representations of divine sound vibrations (mantras) and they are usually based on a square that contains the other geometrical figures; while mandalas are depictions of sacred cosmic dwellings and are based mainly in the use of concentric circles.

Mudras

The word "mudra" comes from the Sanskrit language as follows: "MUD," meaning "joy" and "RA," meaning "to give." The origin of the use of mudras takes place in India. We may describe mudras as specific hand positions that evoke and enclose patterns of cosmic energy and stimulate the flow of certain energy for particular objectives. In other words, they trap cosmic energy within the physical body.

Mudras may be considered as part of a sacred symbolic language that embody spiritual power and facilitates cosmic contact with higher realms, as well as access to elevated states of consciousness. These "seals" of energy stand as a testimony of essential oneness among human beings, the cosmos and Divinity.

Mudras help augment vital energy within the body and therefore, by holding prana within, play a role in cleansing, healing, invigorating and connecting us with our fundamental center. They are specific keys that allow attunement with the cosmos, the activation of certain cosmic forces, and peace of mind. Mudras constitute divine models that represent spiritual vibrations and express sacred ideas.

The hands are essential and very important parts of the human body, being one of the most expressive instruments humans possess. They denote power and serve the purpose of manifesting abilities (work and art), of communicating, of being transmitters of energy, of healing instruments and also are means for spiritual expression, serving as links between humans and Divinity.

The hands can be correlated to polarity as follows:
- The left hand represents the female aspect, the receiving side of the body and is under lunar influence.
- The right hand represents the male aspect, the giving side of the body and is under solar influence.

From the point of view of Ayurveda, each finger represents one of the sacred elements:

Small finger: earth – Annular finger: water – Middle finger: fire – Index finger: air – Thumb: ether

FIGURE #2

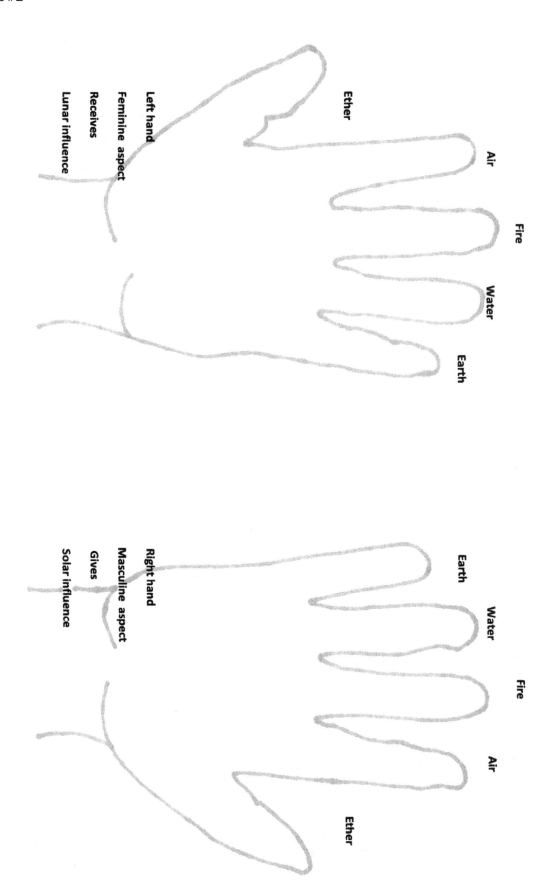

Mudras have been used for:

- Vedic and Tantric rituals.
- Hindu dances.
- In the practice of Hatha Yoga (the asanas or physical postures are a kind of whole body mudras).
- Spiritual offerings.
- Expressions of devotion.
- Welcoming salutations.
- Enhancing certain specific energy influence on the body, with healing purpose.
- Expressing certain feelings.
- Transmitting messages and certain meanings such as bravery, wisdom, compassion, bounty, generosity, etc.
- Bringing about particular states of mind such as peace and wholeness.
- Aiding in meditation by channeling breath energy (concentration) and reproducing an internal arrangement of sacred spaces and vibrations; in other words, invoking divine aspects.

Effects on the Human Body from the Use of Mudras

- Attunement of the physical body to the cosmos, inducing healing and good health.
- They bring about emotional stability.
- They help to achieve a peaceful mind.
- They stimulate spiritual qualities and soul connection.

Mechanism of Action of Mudras

When we assume a certain corporeal position (mudra), it is imprinted in the etheric body. The hand's gestures parallel the closure of an electrical circuit on the nervous system of the person performing them, through which energy circulates vigorously. Thus we may say that mudras exert an effect on the energy system (chakras and energy channels), as well as on the nervous and endocrine systems of the human being, which includes physical, emotional and mental balance and harmony.

Examples of Mudras Used in Meditation and Prayer

1 – VITARKA MUDRA (Discussion) or JNANA MUDRA (Knowledge – Wisdom)

It is performed by uniting the tip of the index finger with the tip of the thumb, while the rest of the fingers are extended. When this mudra is performed with the right hand which is elevated holding the palm outward, it conveys the meaning of "teaching." If it is used in meditation, both hands perform the mudra and they rest on each knee or each thigh with palms upward. The person is sitting cross legged on the floor, or normally on a chair.

The circle that results from the position of the index finger and thumb is a symbol for infinity and perfection. Also, a symbol of the link between the personal self that is represented by the index finger (air), and the Infinite Self represented by the thumb (ether). This mudra facilitates the access to internal knowledge and higher wisdom. It slows down and deepens the breathing and as a consequence of this, it brings about calming of the mind's activity. Also, it increases the blood flow to the brain and augments the lung's capacity.

2 – DHYANA MUDRA (Pose of meditation)

The left hand rests on the lap, palm up and the right hand's dorsum rests on the palm of the left hand with the tips of the thumbs touching each other gently. The right hand represents the sun and the spirit world, while the left hand represents the moon and the material world. The circuit of energy created by this hand's posture produces the following effects:

- Impulses the vital energy (prana) throughout the entire body.
- Stimulates the meditative state by increasing concentration and full awareness.
- Brings about equilibrium between the polarities (mind/body – male/female), helping to transcend duality toward complete oneness.

KECHARI MUDRA

This mudra is considered as the "queen of the mudras" for meditation purposes. It is performed by rolling the tongue upward and backward in a way that it rests against the upper palate and the tip would be pointing toward the location of the pituitary gland within the brain.

This gesture facilitates the rising flow of energy during meditation so that it circulates from the tip of the tongue to the pituitary gland which gets activated and consequently activates the pineal gland to receive light.

ANJALI MUDRA (Offering – Devotion)

This hand posture is made by positioning the fingertips of both hands together, pointing upward and joining the hands at the level of the Heart Chakra. This is a prayer pose that symbolizes the unified being offering its deep devotion.

This mudra represents the union of the right and left sides of the body with the brain and heart (unification). Also, it signifies the union of the spiritual and material worlds at the symbolic altar represented by the heart. This mudra is as well used as a salutation and greeting in India, signifying the recognition of divinity in everyone we meet.

Mantras

The word "mantra" derives from the roots "man" which means mind, or to reflect, and "tran" which means instrument, or salvation. Thus, the general meaning of the word is "instrument of thought." The origin of mantras goes back to ancient "rishis" from India, who contacted higher dimensions to retrieve true teachings and wisdom.

A mantra is a syllable, a word or a phrase which sound contains sacred or spiritual vibrations and meaning. They act as vehicles carrying expressions of divine essence that elevate the mental state of a person and bring about the manifestation of higher levels of consciousness by vivifying divine energy within the individual. Thus, they exert a vibratory and healing effect on the levels of pranic energy and consciousness. They are keys that open access to universal truth.

Mantras are sounds of power that embody truth and represent spiritual reality. The whole cosmos is a vibration ("AUM") originated by the Supreme Source. Thus, through the medium of a mantra, the human being may reach the primordial spiritual center.

Mantras are used in and for:

- Vedic and Tantric rituals.
- Balancing feminine and masculine polarities.
- Empowerment.
- Healing at all levels.
- Awakening the energy centers or chakras.
- Purification.
- Prayer, since mantras are prayers calling forth Divinity.
- Meditation practices.

When used in meditation, the continuous repetition of a mantra charges the air, the breath, the body and the mind with the vibration and energy of the mantra, which evokes higher states of consciousness and transport us to the realm of spirit by expanding our consciousness. So the current of sound vibration floods body and mind, conditioning the subconscious to the pattern of divine perfection represented by the specific mantra and implanting the ideal seed for the germination of a healthy life.

The vibration produced by the chanting of mantras is one of the highest frequencies that prevails and absorbs the lower vibrations, taking the practitioner into accord with the special state symbolized by the mantra. As a result of chanting mantras, an augmented flow of higher intelligence and light reaches the practicing individual. The sound vibration of mantras speaks directly to the soul.

Mantras can be repeated loudly or silently in the mind. The effect is the same, due to the fact that thought is also constituted by pranic energy vibrations. Mantras serve as a means of concentration, direction for the mind, and acceleration of spiritual awakening. Also, this practice is one of reverence and surrendering to God; it conduces to oneness within the self as well as with the entire cosmos and God by raising the consciousness through its resonance.

Examples of Mantras Used in Meditation

Most commonly used mantras are:
- Vija mantras (root or seed mantras)
  These mantras are very powerful and they are composed of one syllable which enwraps the essence of God's energy. Vija mantras correspond to the central energy centers or chakras within the human body and the chanting of these mantras affects strongly the chakra in question; cleansing, activating and bringing more energy to it.
  The correspondences are as follows:
  Base or Root Chakra: "LAM"
  Sacral or Polarity Chakra: "VAM"
                      "RAM"
  Heart Chakra: "YAM"
  Throat Chakra: "HAM"
  Brow or Third Eye Chakra: "OM"
  Crown Chakra: "OM"

"OM" or "AUM" is the primordial and integrated sound of Creation. It represents the ground of cosmic oneness and brilliance, calling forth the divine power and producing a transformation in consciousness that attunes it to Universal Wisdom.

- Unspoken or silent mantra
  This is: "SO HUM" (He I am) and "SA HAM" (She I am).
  This mantra represents the sound of our breath of life. The practice is done by following the respiratory phases silently and mentally repeating "SO" or "SA" while inhaling, and "UM" or "HAM" while exhaling.
- "The Jewel in the Lotus"
  This is: "OM MANI PADME HUM"
  This mantra portrays the energies of compassion, love and wisdom. Its general meaning is a total surrendering to the perfect Will of God: "Let it be the best it could be."
- "OM SHANTI OM"
  This mantra invokes peace.
- Repetition of the names of God
  Any of the names used to refer to God can be chanted and repeated as a mantra.

General and Individual Beneficial Effects of Mantra Chanting

- Cleanses all the human principles or bodies (physical – emotional – mental – soul extension) and lifts the individual from the lower self level to the higher self level.
- Helps the person to become aware of its true nature and the God Force within.
- Activates and regulates energy, with revitalizing effects on the person.
- Calms down chaotic emotions.
- Helps to deal with illness in a more balanced manner and also helps to heal.
- Has a deep effect on the subtle etheric body and the energy centers or chakras by clearing energetic obstructions, destroying retained, crystallized harmful patterns, reinstating a normal flow of vital energy, and preparing the chakras to receive higher forms of energy.
- Brings balance, peace and lucidity to the mind.
- Opens and expands the mind to become receptive to the influx of energy from deeper levels of existence in the cosmos.
- Stimulates the mind to attain higher awareness and creativity.
- Helps to develop the power of concentration and guides the mind to a meditative state.
- Stimulates the development of higher mental functions (abstract thinking, creative imagination, intuition) and the emergence of inner joy.
- Brings spiritual freedom and growth.
- Strengthens the individual and thus helps to improve life conditions.
- By bringing about the corresponding level of spiritual energy it saturates the surrounding environment with it.

All the formerly mentioned aids to meditation can be utilized at unison, or in different combinations, as we choose and prefer.

SYNTHESIS

Aids that can be used to supplement the practice of meditation are:

1 – <u>Yantras</u> ("Instrument" "To hold"): Geometric forms combined in patterns that hold the energy of divine ideas and conduct energy through the dimensions of existence. Diagrammatic expression of a mantra sound.

2 – <u>Mandalas</u> ("Circle"): Type of yantra that represents a sacred pattern or geometrical depiction of the entire cosmos and God the creator at the center.

The sacred geometrical forms used in the construction of yantras and mandalas usually are: circle, triangle and square.

3 – <u>Mudras</u>: Hand postures that evoke and seal patterns of divine cosmic energy in the body. Sacred language embodying spiritual power and facilitating contact with higher realms and higher states of consciousness. Keys to attune to the cosmos and God. The mudras generally used in meditation are:

- Vitarka Mudra ("discussion") or Jnana Mudra ("Knowledge, wisdom")
- Dhyana Mudra ("Meditation")

4 –<u>Mantras</u>: Syllables, words, or phrases that create a resonance which is a spiritual vibration with certain meaning. Vehicles of divine essence that elevate our mental status to levels of higher consciousness. They exert effects on pranic energy and consciousness and can be chanted repeatedly aloud as well as silently in the mind. Sounds of power representing the spiritual reality.

Some of the mantras that can be used in meditation are:

- Vija Mantras (seed mantras): "LAM" "VAM" "RAM" "YAM" "HAM" "OM"
- Silent mantra of the breath: "SO HUM" "SA HAM"
- The "Jewel in the Lotus": "OM MAMI PADME HUM"
- Mantra to invoke peace: "OM SHANTI OM"
- Names of God

CPSIA information can be obtained
at www.ICGtesting.com
Printed in the USA
BVHW022318120620
581411BV00013B/1152